Wonderful ways to prepare

CROCKERY POT DISHES

by JO ANN SHIRLEY

Wonderful ways to prepare

CROCKERY POT DISHES

PLAYMORE INC. NEW YORK USA
UNDER ARRANGEMENT WITH
WALDMAN PUBLISHING CORP.

AYERS & JAMES
SYDNEY AUSTRALIA

STAFFORD PEMBERTON PUBLISHING
KNUTSFORD UNITED KINGDOM

FIRST PUBLISHED 1979

PUBLISHED IN THE USA
BY PLAYMORE INC.
UNDER ARRANGEMENT WITH
WALDMAN PUBLISHING CORP.

PUBLISHED IN AUSTRALIA
BY AYERS & JAMES
CROWS NEST. AUSTRALIA

PUBLISHED IN THE UNITED KINGDOM
BY STAFFORD PEMBERTON PUBLISHING
KNUTSFORD CHESHIRE

ISBN 0 86908 154 3

OVEN TEMPERATURE GUIDE

Description	Gas		Electric		Mark
	C	F	C	F	
Cool	100	200	110	225	¼
Very Slow	120	250	120	250	½
Slow	150	300	150	300	1-2
Moderately slow	160	325	170	340	3
Moderate	180	350	200	400	4
Moderately hot	190	375	220	425	5-6
Hot	200	400	230	450	6-7
Very hot	230	450	250	475	8-9

LIQUID MEASURES

IMPERIAL	METRIC
1 teaspoon	5 ml
1 tablespoon	20 ml
2 fluid ounces (½ cup)	62.5 ml
4 fluid ounces (½ cup)	125 ml
8 fluid ounces (1 cup)	250 ml
1 pint (16 ounces — 2 cups)*	500 ml

* (The imperial pint is equal to 20 fluid ounces.)

SOLID MEASURES

AVOIRDUPOIS	METRIC
1 ounce	30 g
4 ounces (¼ lb)	125 g
8 ounces (½ lb)	250 g
12 ounces (¾ lb)	375 g
16 ounces (1 lb)	500 g
24 ounces (1½ lb)	750 g
32 ounces (2 lb)	1000 g (1 kg)

CUP AND SPOON REPLACEMENTS FOR OUNCES

INGREDIENT	½ oz	1 oz	2 oz	3 oz	4 oz	5 oz	6 oz	7 oz	8 oz
Almonds, ground	2 T	¼ C	½ C	¾ C	1¼ C	1⅓ C	1⅔ C	2 C	2¼ C
slivered	6 t	¼ C	½ C	¾ C	1 C	1⅓ C	1⅔ C	2 C	2¼ C
whole	2 T	¼ C	⅓ C	½ C	¾ C	1 C	1¼ C	1⅓ C	1½ C
Apples, dried whole	3 T	½ C	1 C	1⅓ C	2 C	2⅓ C	2¾ C	3⅓ C	3¾ C
Apricots, chopped	2 T	¼ C	½ C	¾ C	1 C	1¼ C	1½ C	1¾ C	2 C
whole	2 T	3 T	½ C	⅔ C	1 C	1¼ C	1⅓ C	1½ C	1¾ C
Arrowroot	1 T	2 T	⅓ C	½ C	⅔ C	¾ C	1 C	1¼ C	1⅓ C
Baking Powder	1 T	2 T	⅓ C	½ C	⅔ C	¾ C	1 C	1 C	1¼ C
Baking Soda	1 T	2 T	⅓ C	½ C	⅔ C	¾ C	1 C	1 C	1¼ C
Barley	1 T	2 T	¼ C	½ C	⅔ C	¾ C	1 C	1 C	1¼ C
Breadcrumbs, dry	2 T	¼ C	½ C	¾ C	1 C	1¼ C	1½ C	1¾ C	2 C
soft	¼ C	½ C	1 C	1½ C	2 C	2½ C	3 C	3⅔ C	4¼ C
Biscuit Crumbs	2 T	¼ C	½ C	¾ C	1¼ C	1⅓ C	1⅔ C	2 C	2¼ C
Butter	3 t	6 t	¼ C	⅓ C	½ C	⅔ C	¾ C	1 C	1 C
Cheese, grated, lightly packed,									
natural cheddar	6 t	¼ C	½ C.	¾ C	1 C	1¼ C	1½ C	1¾ C	2 C
Processed cheddar	5 t	2 T	⅓ C	⅔ C	¾ C	1 C	1¼ C	1½ C	1⅔ C
Parmesan, Romano	6 t	¼ C	½ C	¾ C	1 C	1⅓ C	1⅔ C	2 C	2¼ C
Cherries, candied, chopped	1 T	2 T	⅓ C	½ C	¾ C	1 C	1 C	1⅓ C	1½ C
whole	1 T	2 T	⅓ C	½ C	⅔ C	¾ C	1 C	1¼ C	1⅓ C
Cocoa	2 T	¼ C	½ C	¾ C	1¼ C	1⅓ C	1⅔ C	2 C	2¼ C
Coconut, desiccated	2 T	⅓ C	⅔ C	1 C	1⅓ C	1⅔ C	2 C	2⅓ C	2⅔ C
shredded	⅓ C	⅔ C	1¼ C	1¾ C	2½ C	3 C	3⅔ C	4⅓ C	5 C
Cornstarch	6 t	3 T	½ C	⅔ C	1 C	1¼ C	1½ C	1⅔ C	2 C
Corn Syrup	2 t	1 T	2 T	¼ C	⅓ C	½ C	½ C	⅔ C	⅔ C
Coffee, ground	2 T	⅓ C	⅔ C	1 C	1⅓ C	1⅔ C	2 C	2⅓ C	2⅔ C
instant	3 T	½ C	1 C	1⅓ C	1¾ C	2¼ C	2⅔ C	3 C	3½ C
Cornflakes	½ C	1 C	2 C	3 C	4¼ C	5¼ C	6¼ C	7⅓C	8⅓ C
Cream of Tartar	1 T	2 T	⅓ C	½ C	⅔ C	¾ C	1 C	1 C	1¼ C
Currants	1 T	2 T	⅓ C	⅔ C	¾ C	1 C	1¼ C	1½ C	1⅔ C
Custard Powder	6 t	3 T	½ C	⅔ C	1 C	1¼ C	1½ C	1⅔ C	2 C
Dates, chopped	1 T	2 T	⅓ C	⅔ C	¾ C	1 C	1¼ C	1½ C	1⅔ C
whole, pitted	1 T	2 T	⅓ C	½ C	¾ C	1 C	1¼ C	1⅓ C	1½ C
Figs, chopped	1 T	2 T	⅓ C	½ C	¾ C	1 C	1 C	1⅓ C	1½ C
Flour, all-purpose or cake	6 t	¼ C	½ C	¾ C	1 C	1¼ C	1½ C	1¾ C	2 C
wholemeal	6 t	3 T	½ C	⅔ C	1 C	1¼ C	1⅓ C	1⅔ C	1¾ C
Fruit, mixed	1 T	2 T	⅓ C	½ C	¾ C	1 C	1¼ C	1⅓ C	1½ C
Gelatin	5 t	2 T	⅓ C	½ C	¾ C	1 C	1 C	1¼ C	1½ C
Ginger, crystallised pieces	1 T	2 T	⅓ C	½ C	¾ C	1 C	1¼ C	1⅓ C	1½ C
ground	6 t	⅓ C	½ C	¾ C	1¼ C	1½ C	1¾ C	2 C	2¼ C
preserved, heavy syrup	1 T	2 T	⅓ C	½ C	⅔ C	¾ C	1 C	1 C	1¼ C
Glucose, liquid	2 t	1 T	2 T	¼ C	⅓ C	½ C	½ C	⅔ C	⅔ C
Haricot Beans	1 T	2 T	⅓ C	½ C	⅔ C	¾ C	1 C	1 C	1¼ C

In this table, t represents teaspoonful, T represents tablespoonful and C represents cupful.

CUP AND SPOON REPLACEMENTS FOR OUNCES (Cont.)

INGREDIENT	½ oz	1 oz	2 oz	3 oz	4 oz	5 oz	6 oz	7 oz	8 oz
Honey	2 t	1 T	2 T	¼ C	⅓ C	½ C	½ C	⅔ C	⅔ C
Jam	2 t	1 T	2 T	¼ C	⅓ C	½ C	½ C	⅔ C	¾ C
Lentils	1 T	2 T	⅓ C	½ C	⅔ C	¾ C	1 C	1 C	1¼ C
Macaroni (see pasta)									
Milk Powder, full cream	2 T	¼ C	½ C	¾ C	1¼ C	1⅓ C	1⅔ C	2 C	2¼ C
non fat	2 T	⅓ C	¾ C	1¼ C	1½ C	2 C	2⅓ C	2¾ C	3¼ C
Nutmeg	6 t	3 T	½ C	⅔ C	¾ C	1 C	1¼ C	1½ C	1⅔ C
Nuts, chopped	6 t	¼ C	½ C	¾ C	1 C	1¼ C	1½ C	1¾ C	2 C
Oatmeal	1 T	2 T	½ C	⅔ C	¾ C	1 C	1¼ C	1½ C	1⅔ C
Olives, whole	1 T	2 T	⅓ C	⅔ C	¾ C	1 C	1¼ C	1½ C	1⅔ C
sliced	1 T	2 T	⅓ C	⅔ C	¾ C	1 C	1¼ C	1½ C	1⅔ C
Pasta, short (e.g. macaroni)	1 T	2 T	⅓ C	⅔ C	¾ C	1 C	1¼ C	1½ C	1⅔ C
Peaches, dried & whole	1 T	2 T	⅓ C	⅔ C	¾ C	1 C	1¼ C	1½ C	1⅔ C
chopped	6 t	¼ C	½ C	¾ C	1 C	1¼ C	1½ C	1¾ C	2 C
Peanuts, shelled, raw, whole	1 T	2 T	⅓ C	½ C	¾ C	1 C	1¼ C	1⅓ C	1½ C
roasted	1 T	2 T	⅓ C	⅔ C	¾ C	1 C	1¼ C	1½ C	1⅔ C
Peanut Butter	3 t	6 t	3 T	⅓ C	½ C	½ C	⅔ C	¾ C	1 C
Peas, split	1 T	2 T	⅓ C	½ C	⅔ C	¾ C	1 C	1 C	1¼ C
Peel, mixed	1 T	2 T	⅓ C	½ C	¾ C	1 C	1 C	1¼ C	1½ C
Potato, powder	1 T	2 T	¼ C	⅓ C	½ C	⅔ C	¾ C	1 C	1¼ C
flakes	¼ C	½ C	1 C	1⅓ C	2 C	2⅓ C	2¾ C	3⅓ C	3¾ C
Prunes, chopped	1 T	2 T	⅓ C	½ C	⅔ C	¾ C	1 C	1¼ C	1⅓ C
whole pitted	1 T	2 T	⅓ C	½ C	⅔ C	¾ C	1 C	1 C	1¼ C
Raisins	2 T	¼ C	⅓ C	½ C	¾ C	1 C	1 C	1⅓ C	1½ C
Rice, short grain, raw	1 T	2 T	¼ C	½ C	⅔ C	¾ C	1 C	1 C	1¼ C
long grain, raw	1 T	2 T	⅓ C	½ C	¾ C	1 C	1¼ C	1⅓ C	1½ C
Rice Bubbles	⅔ C	1¼ C	2½ C	3⅔ C	5 C	6¼ C	7½ C	8¾ C	10 C
Rolled Oats	2 T	⅓ C	⅔ C	1 C	1⅓ C	1¾ C	2 C	2½ C	2¾ C
Sago	2 T	¼ C	⅓ C	½ C	¾ C	1 C	1 C	1¼ C	1½ C
Salt, common	3 t	6 t	¼ C	⅓ C	½ C	⅔ C	¾ C	1 C	1 C
Semolina	1 T	2 T	⅓ C	½ C	¾ C	1 C	1 C	1⅓ C	1½ C
Spices	6 t	3 T	¼ C	⅓ C	½ C	½ C	⅔ C	¾ C	1 C
Sugar, plain	3 t	6 t	¼ C	⅓ C	½ C	⅔ C	¾ C	1 C	1 C
confectioners'	1 T	2 T	⅓ C	½ C	¾ C	1 C	1 C	1¼ C	1½ C
moist brown	1 T	2 T	⅓ C	½ C	¾ C	1 C	1 C	1⅓ C	1½ C
Tapioca	1 T	2 T	⅓ C	½ C	⅔ C	¾ C	1 C	1¼ C	1⅓ C
Treacle	2 t	1 T	2 T	¼ C	⅓ C	½ C	½ C	⅔ C	⅔ C
Walnuts, chopped	2 T	¼ C	½ C	¾ C	1 C	1¼ C	1½ C	1¾ C	2 C
halved	2 T	⅓ C	⅔ C	1 C	1¼ C	1½ C	1¾ C	2¼ C	2½ C
Yeast, dried	6 t	3 T	½ C	⅔ C	1 C	1¼ C	1⅓ C	1⅔ C	1¾ C
compressed	3 t	6 t	3 T	⅓ C	½ C	½ C	⅔ C	¾ C	1 C

In this table, t represents teaspoonful, T represents tablespoonful and C represents cupful.

Contents

Soups

Haricot Bean Soup

1½ cups haricot beans
5 cups (1¼ liters) water
2 medium onions, chopped
2 medium carrots, chopped
1 stalk celery, chopped
4 tablespoons oil

2 cloves garlic, minced
1 bay leaf
1 ham bone
1½ teaspoons salt
¼ teaspoon black pepper
chopped parsley

1. Soak the beans in the water overnight. Transfer to a saucepan and simmer in the same water for about 1½ hours. Put the beans and the water in the crockery pot.
2. Saute the onions, carrots and celery in the oil until the onions are transparent. Put into the crockery pot.
3. Add the garlic, bay leaf, ham bone, salt, pepper and two more cups of water. Cover and cook on the low setting (200°F 100°C) for 6-8 hours.
4. Serve sprinkled with parsley.

Serves 6-8.

Eastern Meat Ball Soup

⅓ cup lentils
1 medium onion, chopped
2 small carrots, chopped
1 stalk celery, chopped
2½ tablespoons oil
½ lb (250 g) tomatoes
1 teaspoon grated fresh ginger
1 teaspoon salt
½ teaspoon cumin

¼ teaspoon pepper
6 cups (1½ liters) beef stock
1 lb (500 g) ground lamb
⅓ cup (85 ml) chicken stock
4 tablespoons plain flour
1 teaspoon salt
1 clove garlic, minced
1½ tablespoons chopped parsley

1. Put lentils in a saucepan with enough water to cover. **Bring to a boil and** boil for three minutes. Remove from heat and allow to stand for one hour. Return to the heat and simmer for one hour. Add a little more water if necessary. Drain.
2. Saute the onion, carrots and celery in the oil until the onion is transparent. Put into the crockery pot.
3. Add the lentils, tomatoes, ginger, salt, cumin, pepper and beef stock. Cover and cook on the low setting (200°F — 100°C) for four hours.
4. Mix together the ground lamb, chicken stock, flour, salt, garlic and parsley. Form into small balls and drop into the soup. Cook for another 45 minutes.

Serves 6.

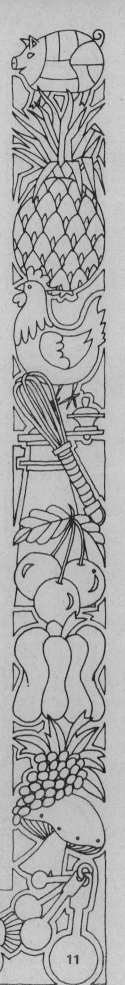

Quick and Easy Mixed Soup

1 teaspoon curry powder
2 teaspoons butter
1 can tomato soup
1 can green pea soup
1 can consomme

3 cups (750 ml) water
4 tablespoons sherry
salt and pepper
chopped chives

1. Heat the crockery pot to the high setting (300°F — 150°C).
2. Mix together the curry powder and butter and melt in the crockery pot. Cook for two minutes.
3. Mix together the tomato soup, pea soup and consomme and put into the crockery pot.
4. Stir in the water, cover and cook on the high setting until hot.
5. Stir in the sherry and season to taste with salt and pepper.
6. Serve sprinkled with chopped chives.

Serves 6-8.

Cream of Corn Soup

4 teaspoons (20 g) butter
4 teaspoons plain flour
1 cup (250 ml) milk
1 can (440 g) corn kernels
2 cups (500 ml) chicken stock
2½ tablespoons chopped celery

1½ tablespoons chopped onion
1 teaspoon Worcestershire
    sauce
2 cups (500 ml) milk
salt and pepper
slivered almonds

1. Melt the butter in a small saucepan. Stir in the flour and cook over a low heat for one minute.
2. Slowly add the milk, stirring constantly, until thick and smooth.
3. Drain the corn and add to the white sauce.
4. Put the corn mixture, chicken stock, celery, onion and Worcestershire sauce in the crockery pot and cook on the low setting (200°F—100°C) for two hours.
5. Add the milk and salt and pepper to taste. Mix well and heat through.
6. Serve garnished with slivered almonds.

Serves 4-6.

Yellow Split Pea Soup

1 cup yellow split peas	1 medium onion, chopped
1 ham bone	¼ lb (125 g) diced ham
8 cups (2 liters) water	salt and pepper
½ teaspoon dry mustard	2½ tablespoons sherry
3 medium carrots, chopped	
4 tablespoons chopped parsley	

1. Soak the peas in enough water to cover for several hours. Drain.
2. Put the peas in the crockery pot with the ham bone, water, mustard, carrots, parsley and onion.
3. Cover and cook on the low setting (200°F — 100°C) for 8-10 hours.
4. Remove the ham bone and cut off any meat. Dice the meat and return to the soup.
5. Add the ham, salt and pepper to taste and the sherry to the soup and heat thoroughly.

Serves 6-8.

Mexican Soup

1 lb (500 g) lean ground beef
8 cups (2 liters) chicken stock
4 tablespoons plain flour
1 egg
1 red chilli pepper
4 medium carrots, grated
5½ tablespoons rice

½ lb (250 g) spinach, shredded
½ teaspoon oregano
¼ lb (125 g) ham, chopped
2½ tablespoons chopped parsley
lemon wedges

1. Mix together the ground beef, ½ cup stock, flour and egg. Form into small balls. Set aside.
2. Put the remaining stock, chilli pepper, carrots and rice in the crockery pot on the high setting (300°F —150°C).
3. When the stock is simmering, add the meat balls, cover and cook for ½ hour.
4. Turn the heat to low (200°F — 100°C) and cook for three hours.
5. Add the spinach, oregano, ham and parsley, cover and cook for 20 minutes.
6. Serve with lemon wedges.

Serves 6-8.

13

French Onion Soup

1 lb (500 g) brown onions, sliced
4 tablespoons (60 g) butter
4 cups (1 liter) beef stock
1 cup (250 ml) white wine
¼ cup (65 ml) sherry
1½ teaspoons Worcestershire sauce
1 clove garlic, minced
rounds of toasted French bread
½ cup grated cheese

1. Saute the onion in the butter until transparent.
2. Put into the crockery pot with the stock, wine, sherry, Worchestershire sauce, and garlic. Cover and cook on the low setting (200°F—100°) for 6-8 hours.
3. Put a round of toast in each soup bowl and pour the soup over it.
4. Sprinkle with cheese and put into a hot oven or under a broiler until the cheese melts.

Serves 4-6.

Beef and Vegetable Soup

2½ tablespoons oil
1½ lb (750 g) stewing beef
1 medium onion, chopped
2 medium carrots, chopped
1 green pepper, chopped
2 stalks celery, sliced
8 cups (2 liters) beef stock
1 lb (500 g) tomatoes, chopped
salt and pepper
½ teaspoon oregano

1. Cut the beef into small pieces and saute in a frypan until well browned. Transfer to crockery pot.
2. Saute the onion until transparent in the frypan.
3. Add the carrots, pepper and celery and cook for five minutes. Put in crockery pot.
4. Stir in the beef stock, tomatoes, salt and pepper to taste and oregano.
5. Cover and cook on low heat (200°F —100°C) for 8-12 hours.

Serves 8.

Onion Soup

3 chicken wings
1 medium onion, chopped
2½ cups (625 ml) chicken stock
1 bay leaf
1½ teaspoons thyme
2 teaspoons salt
½ teaspoon pepper

6 medium onions, thinly sliced
3 tablespoons (45 g) butter
4 tablespoons plain flour
½ teaspoon dry mustard
3 cups (750 ml) milk
½ teaspoon coriander
chopped parsley

1. Put the chicken wings, onion, chicken stock, bay leaf, thyme, salt and pepper in the crockery pot.
2. Cover and cook on the low setting (200°F — 100°C) for six to eight hours. Remove the chicken wings and the bay leaf.
3. Saute the onions in the butter in a large frypan until the onions are golden brown.
4. Stir in the flour and mustard and one cup (250 ml) of the liquid from the crockery pot. Stir until smooth and thick.
5. Add the milk slowly, stirring constantly. Mix in the coriander.
6. Pour into the crockery pot and heat on the high setting (300°F—150°C) for a few minutes.
7. Serve garnished with chopped parsley.

Serves 4-6.

Vegetable Soup

2 medium onions, chopped	1 cup diced celery
4 teaspoons (20 g) butter	1½ tablespoons tomato paste
6 cups (1½ liters) beef stock	2 teaspoons salt
4 medium carrots, diced	¼ teaspoon pepper
1 turnip, diced	¼ teaspoon basil
3 medium potatoes, diced	
2½ tablespoons chopped parsley	

1. Saute the onions in the butter until transparent.
2. Add half a cup of the beef stock to the onions and cook over a low heat for one minute scraping the bottom of the pan. Put into the crockery pot.
3. Add the rest of the beef stock and the remaining ingredients and mix well.
4. Cover and cook on the low setting (200°F — 100°C) for six to eight hours.

Serves 4-6.

Vichyssoise

6 large or 9 small leeks	3 cups diced potatoes
3 tablespoons (45 g) butter	3 teaspoons salt
1 small onion, minced	1¼ cups (300 ml) cream
4 cups (1 liter) chicken stock	chopped chives

1. Wash the leeks very carefully removing the outer leaves and the green leaves. Cut in half.
2. Saute the onion in the butter until transparent.
3. Add half a cup of the chicken stock to the onion and cook for one minute over a low heat scraping the bottom of the pan. Put into the crockery pot.
4. Put the remaining chicken stock in the crockery pot with the potatoes, salt and leeks.
5. Cover and cook on the low setting (200°F — 100°C) for five to seven hours.
6. Press the soup through a strainer or puree in an electric blender.
7. Stir in the cream and serve hot or cold garnished with chopped chives.

Serves 4-6.

Cabbage and Beef Soup

1½ lb (750 g) round steak, cut into cubes
2½ tablespoons oil
4 cups (1 liter) water
4 teaspoons soy sauce
4 cups shredded cabbage
2 medium onions, chopped
1 clove garlic, minced

¼ lb (125 g) bacon, chopped
1½ teaspoons salt
½ teaspoon pepper
½ teaspoon dry mustard
¼ lb (125 g) diced potatoes
¼ lb (125 g) diced sweet potatoes
1½ tablespoons tomato paste

1. Saute the meat in the oil until well browned on all sides. Put into the crockery pot.
2. Add the remaining ingredients and mix well.
3. Cover and cook on the low setting (200°F — 100°C) for six to eight hours.

Serves 6.

Corn Chowder

¼ lb (125 g) bacon, chopped
2 medium onions, chopped
3 cups diced potatoes
1½ cups corn kernels
2 cups (500 ml) water

2 teaspoons salt
¼ teaspoon pepper
⅛ teaspoon paprika
1 cup (250 ml) milk
1 cup (250 ml) cream

1. Fry the bacon in a frypan until crisp. Remove the bacon and set aside.
2. Saute the onions in the bacon fat until transparent. Put into the crockery pot.
3. Add the potatoes, corn, water, salt, pepper and paprika to the crockery pot.
4. Cover and cook on the low setting (200°F — 100°C) for six to eight hours.
5. Before serving add the milk and the cream and heat through.

Serves 6.

Beef Soup

1 lb (500 g) chuck steak, diced	6 peppercorns
4 teaspoons (20 g) butter	2½ tablespoons chopped parsley
1 tablespoon (20 g) butter	½ teaspoon thyme
8 cups (2 liters) beef stock	2 cloves garlic, minced
2 medium carrots, coarsely chopped	½ cup (125 ml) red wine
3 medium onions, quartered	chopped chives

1. Sprinkle the salt on the meat and brown the meat in the butter in a frypan.
2. Add one cup of the beef stock to the meat and cook over a low heat for two minutes, scraping the bottom of the frypan. Put into the crockery pot.
3. Add the rest of the ingredients except the wine and chives. Mix well.
4. Cover and cook on the low setting (200°F — 100°C) for ten to twelve hours.
5. Turn the crockery pot to the high setting (300°F — 150°C) and stir in the wine. Simmer, uncovered, for about five minutes.
6. Serve garnished with chopped chives.

Serves 4-6.

Carrot Soup

4 chicken wings or 4 necks
1 medium onion, chopped
2½ cups (625 ml) chicken
  stock
1 bay leaf
1 teaspoon thyme
2½ teaspoons salt

½ teaspoon pepper
4 cloves
3 tablespoons (45 g) butter
3 cups thinly sliced carrots
1 cup (250 ml) cream
chopped chives

1. Put the chicken wings or necks, onion, chicken stock, bay leaf, thyme, salt, pepper and cloves into the crockery pot.
2. Cover and cook on the low setting (200°F — 100°C) for six to eight hours. Discard the chicken, bay leaf and cloves.
3. Saute the carrots in the butter in a large frypan for about ten minutes.
4. Put the carrots in the crockery pot and cook on the high setting (300°F — 150°C) until tender.
5. Put the carrot mixture through a sieve or puree in an electric blender.
6. Stir in the cream and serve immediately.
7. Garnish with chopped chives.

Serves 4-6.

Lentil Soup

1½ cups lentils
5 cups (1¼ liters) water
1 medium onion, chopped
1 medium carrot, chopped
1 stalk celery, chopped
2½ tablespoons chopped parsley
4 tablespoons oil
1 bay leaf

2 cloves garlic, minced
1½ teaspoons salt
½ teaspoon black pepper
½ teaspoon oregano
4 teaspoons tomato paste
½ cup (125 ml) strong beef stock
4 tablespoons wine vinegar

1. Soak the lentils in enough water to cover for several hours. Drain.
2. Mix the drained lentils and the five cups of water in a saucepan and bring to the boil. Reduce heat and simmer for one hour. Put into the crockery pot.
3. Saute the onion, carrot, celery and parsley in the oil until the onion is transparent. Put into the crockery pot.
4. Add the bay leaf, garlic, salt, pepper, oregano and the tomato paste mixed with the beef stock to the lentils. Mix well.
5. Cover the crockery pot and cook on the low setting (200°F — 100°C) for 6-8 hours.
6. Add the vinegar, mix thoroughly and cook on the high setting (300°F — 150°C) for ½ hour.

Serves 6-8.

Split Pea Soup

3 tablespoons (45 g) butter
2 medium onions, minced
8 cups (2 liters) water
2 cups dried split peas
5 cloves
1 bay leaf

½ lb (250 g) bacon bones
2 stalks celery, chopped
2 medium carrots, diced
¼ teaspoon marjoram
1 tablespoon salt
½ teaspoon pepper

1. Put all the ingredients into the crockery pot.
2. Cover and cook on the low setting (200°F — 100°C) for eight to ten hours.
3. Before serving remove the bacon bones, bay leaf and cloves.

Serves 6-8.

Mulligatawny Soup

1 cup (250 ml) boiling water	1 chicken
1 cup desiccated coconut	4 cups (1 liter) chicken stock
1 medium onion, chopped	1 bay leaf
1 medium carrot, grated	salt and pepper
4 tablespoons (60 g) butter	cooked rice
curry powder to taste	lemon wedges

1. Pour the boiling water over the coconut and allow to stand for 15 minutes.
2. Saute the onion and the carrot in the butter until the onion is transparent.
3. Add the curry powder and cook for five minutes.
4. Remove the chicken meat from the skin and bones. Cut into small pieces and add to the onion and carrot mixture. Cook until the chicken is browned.
5. Transfer the mixture to the crockery pot.
6. Strain the coconut mixture and add the liquid to the chicken with the chicken stock and bay leaf. Discard the coconut.
7. Season to taste with salt and pepper, cover and cook on the high setting (300°F —150°C) for three hours.
8. Serve the soup over cooked rice and garnish with lemon wedges.

Serves 4.

Meat

Creamy Meat Balls

¼ cup (65 g) butter
1 medium onion, chopped
2 lb (1 kg) ground beef
2 eggs
2 teaspoons salt
½ teaspoon pepper
¼ teaspoon tarragon
¼ teaspoon marjoram
2½ tablespoons plain flour

5½ tablespoons tomato paste
¾ cup (185 ml) beef stock
4 teaspoons Worcestershire sauce
2 teaspoons vinegar
½ lb (250 g) mushrooms, sliced
1 cup (250 g) sour cream

1. Saute the onion in half the butter in a large frypan until golden brown. Put the onion in the crockery pot.
2. Mix together the beef, eggs, salt and pepper. Form into small balls.
3. Brown the meat balls in the same frypan.
4. Sprinkle on the tarragon, marjoram and flour. Shake the frypan to turn the meat balls and coat them with the flour. Put into the crockery pot.
5. Mix together the tomato paste, beef stock, Worcestershire sauce and vinegar in the frypan. Scrape the bottom of the pan and cook for two minutes. Pour over the meat balls.
6. Cover the crockery pot and cook on the low setting (200°F—100°C) for about 1½ hours.
7. Melt the remaining butter and saute the mushrooms for five minutes.
8. Add the mushrooms and the sour cream to the meat balls and heat through.

Serves 6.

Spinach Meat Balls

1 lb (500 g) spinach	½ lb (250 g) ground pork
3 eggs	1 medium onion, minced
3 slices bread, crust removed	plain flour
5½ tablespoons Parmesan cheese	salt and pepper
2 teaspoons salt	3 tablespoons (45 g) butter
½ teaspoon black pepper	½ cup (125 ml) consomme
2 cloves garlic, minced	½ cup (125 ml) red wine
1½ lb (750 g) ground beef	½ teaspoon oregano
	chopped chives

1. Cut the coarse white stem from the spinach. Wash the spinach several times and chop finely. Cook in a covered saucepan with no added water until the spinach is limp. Drain and squeeze dry.
2. Beat the eggs and add the bread (shredded), cheese, salt, pepper and garlic.
3. Add the beef, pork and onion and mix thoroughly.
4. Form the mixture into small balls and roll in the flour seasoned with salt and pepper.
5. Melt the butter in a large frypan and brown the meat balls. When brown, transfer to the crockery pot.
6. Pour the consomme and red wine into the frypan. Add the oregano and scrape the bottom of the pan and boil rapidly to reduce the liquid to about ½ cup. Pour over the meat balls.
7. Cover the crockery pot and cook on the low setting (200°F — 100°C) for 1½ hours.
8. Serve sprinkled with chopped chives.

Serves 6.

Corned Beef

4 lb (2 kg) corned beef	3 medium onions, quartered
4 medium carrots, cut in large pieces	1½ cups (375 ml) white wine
3 stalks celery, thickly sliced	1 bay leaf
	5 cloves

1. Rinse the meat thoroughly under cold running water. Place in the crockery pot.
2. Put the vegetables in the crockery pot with the wine, bay leaf and cloves.
3. Cover and cook on the low setting (200°F — 100°C) for eight hours.

(Any meat leftover from this dish may, of course, be eaten cold.)

Serves 10.

Eastern Pot Roast

4 lb (2 kg) chuck steak (in one piece)	¼ teaspoon pepper
4 tablespoons oil	1 medium onion, chopped
3 cloves garlic, minced	1 small carrot, chopped
1 cup (250 ml) sherry	4 cloves
¼ cup (65 ml) soy sauce	1½ tablespoons chopped parsley
2 teaspoons grated fresh ginger	

1. Mix together one tablespoon of the oil and the minced garlic. Rub on the roast and place the meat into a large bowl.
2. Mix together the sherry, soy sauce, ginger, pepper, onion, carrot, cloves and parsley and pour over the meat. Allow to marinate overnight in the refrigerator.
3. Remove the meat from the marinade. Strain the marinade and reserve one cup.
4. Heat the remaining oil and brown the meat on all sides. Put into the crockery pot.
5. Pour on ½ cup reserved marinade, cover and cook on the low setting (200°F — 100°C) for eight hours. Remove from crockery pot and keep warm.
6. Turn the heat to the high setting (300°F — 150°C) and add the remaining marinade. Boil rapidly until reduced slightly.
7. Carve the meat and pour the sauce over it.

Serves 8-10.

Walnut Beef

2 lb (1 kg) rump steak, cubed	3 cloves garlic, minced
¼ cup plain flour	¼ cup (65 ml) vinegar
salt and pepper	¼ teaspoon cinnamon
4 tablespoons oil	¼ teaspoon ground cloves
1 cup (250 ml) water	½ cup ground walnuts
¼ cup (65 ml) tomato paste	1½ tablespoons lemon juice

1. Toss the meat in the flour seasoned with salt and pepper.
2. Brown the meat thoroughly in the oil in a large frypan. Put the meat in the crockery pot.
3. Mix the water with the tomato paste and add to the frypan. Scrape the bottom of the frypan and cook over a low heat for one minute. Pour over the meat in the crockery pot and mix well.
4. Add the garlic, vinegar, cinnamon and cloves. Mix thoroughly.
5. Cover the pot and cook on the low setting (200°F — 100°C) for eight hours.
6. Before serving add the walnuts and lemon juice and heat through.

Serves 6.

Braised Ribs

4 lb (2 kg) beef short ribs, in 3-inch (8-cm) lengths	4 tablespoons soy sauce
2 medium onions, chopped	2½ tablespoons vinegar
4 teaspoons (20 g) butter	2½ tablespoons brown sugar
⅔ cup (185 ml) barbecue sauce	

1. Put the ribs in a 475°F (250°C) oven for fifteen minutes. Drain off the fat and put the ribs into the crockery pot.
2. Saute the onions in the butter in a small frypan until the onions are golden brown.
3. Add the barbecue sauce, soy sauce, vinegar and brown sugar. Mix well and cook over a low heat for two minutes.
4. Pour the sauce over the meat, cover and cook on the low setting (200°F — 100°C) for eight hours.

Serves 4-5.

Beef Stew with Red Wine

2 lb (1 kg) chuck steak, cubed	½ teaspoon black pepper
¼ lb (125 g) bacon, diced	½ teaspoon rosemary
4 medium onions, chopped	2 teaspoons grated orange rind
4 teaspoons vinegar	
4 teaspoons brown sugar	2½ tablespoons cornstarch
1½ cups (375 ml) red wine	2½ tablespoons water
2 teaspoons salt	chopped parsley

1. Saute the meat in a frypan with the bacon and onions until the meat is well browned. Put into the crockery pot with the bacon and onions.
2. Mix together the vinegar, brown sugar and red wine. Pour into the frypan, scrape the bottom and cook over a low heat for one minute.
3. Mix the salt, pepper, rosemary and orange rind with the wine mixture and pour over the meat.
4. Cover the crockery pot and cook on the low setting (200°F —100°C) for eight hours.
5. Mix the cornstarch with the water.
6. Turn the crockery pot to the high setting (300°F — 150°C).
7. Add the cornstarch and stir until the sauce is thick.
8. Serve garnished with chopped parsley.

Serves 6.

Swiss Steak

2 lb (1 kg) round steak
¼ cup plain flour
2 teaspoons dry mustard
1½ teaspoons salt
½ teaspoon black pepper
3 tablespoons (45 g) butter
2½ tablespoons oil
1 medium onion, minced

2 medium carrots, grated
2 stalks celery, chopped
1 lb (500 g) tomatoes, chopped
2 tablespoons Worcestershire sauce
3 teaspoons brown sugar

1. Cut the steak into six equal portions.
2. Mix together the flour, mustard, salt and pepper. Coat the steaks thoroughly with this flour mixture.
3. Brown the steak in half the butter and oil. Put the steaks in the crockery pot.
4. Heat the remaining butter and oil and saute the onion, carrots and celery until the onion is transparent.
5. Add the tomatoes, Worcestershire sauce and brown sugar. Cook for three minutes.
6. Pour the vegetables over the meat with the liquid and cook, covered, on the low setting (200°F — 100°C) for about eight hours.

Serves 6.

Swedish Meat Balls

2 lb (1 kg) ground beef
1 medium onion, minced
2 eggs
½ cup oatmeal
⅔ cup (165 ml) milk
2½ tablespoons chopped parsley

1 teaspoon salt
½ teaspoon black pepper
½ teaspoon nutmeg
½ cup (125 ml) beef stock
yoghurt

1. Mix together the beef, onion, eggs, oatmeal, milk, parsley, salt, pepper and nutmeg. Shape into small balls. Place on a baking tray and bake in a 450°F (230°C) oven for about 15 minutes. Put into the crockery pot.
2. Pour the beef stock over the meat balls.
3. Cover and cook on the low setting (200°F — 100°C) for 1½ hours.
4. Serve with yoghurt spooned on top.

Serves 6.

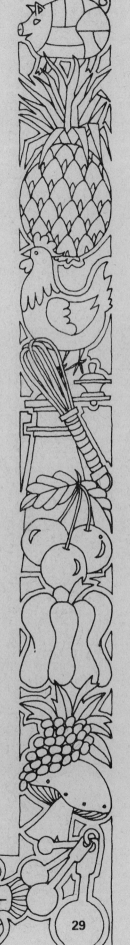

Ginger Steak

3 stalks celery, sliced
2 medium onions, chopped
4 tablespoons (60 g) butter
2 lb (1 kg) topside steak, cut
    into six pieces
¼ cup (65 ml) soy sauce

½ cup (125 ml) red wine
¼ teaspoon pepper
2 teaspoons grated fresh
    ginger
½ lb (250 g) mushrooms,
    sliced

1. Saute the celery and onions in one tablespoon of butter until the onions are transparent. Remove from frypan.
2. Add one more tablespoon of butter to the frypan and brown the steaks on both sides. Put the meat into the crockery pot.
3. Combine the soy sauce and red wine in the frypan and scrape the bits from the bottom. Pour over the meat.
4. Sprinkle the pepper and ginger over the meat.
5. Add the celery and onions to the meat.
6. Cover and cook on the low setting (200°F — 100°C) for seven hours.
7. Saute the mushrooms in the remaining butter and add to the crockery pot ½ hour before the end of the cooking time. Serves 6.

Bolonaise Sauce

2 medium onions, minced
2 medium carrots, minced
2 stalks celery, chopped
1 clove garlic, minced
¼ cup (65 ml) oil
3 lb (1½ kg) ground beef
1 lb (500 g) tomatoes,
    chopped

1 cup (250 ml) red wine
2 teaspoons oregano
2½ tablespoons tomato paste
salt and pepper
½ cup (125 ml) cream

1. Saute the onions, carrots, celery and garlic in the oil in a large frypan until the onions are transparent. Put into the crockery pot.
2. Brown the meat in the same frypan stirring with a fork to break up the meat. Put into the crockery pot with the tomatoes, red wine, oregano, tomato paste, and salt and pepper to taste. Stir well.
3. Cover and cook on the low setting (200°F — 100°C) for eight hours. Skim any fat off the top.
4. Add the cream, stir well and cook on the high setting (300°F — 150°C), uncovered, until the sauce is reduced and thick. Serves 8.

Noodle Meat Casserole

1 lb (500 g) spinach	4 tablespoons tomato paste
½ lb (250 g) noodles	2 teaspoons salt
1 lb (500 g) ground meat	1 teaspoon basil
½ lb (250 g) Italian sausage	½ cup grated Parmesan
1 medium onion, minced	cheese
2½ tablespoons oil	1 cup (250 g) sour cream
1 lb (500 g) tomatoes,	1 cup grated cheddar cheese
chopped	chopped chives

1. Cut the white stem from the spinach. Wash thoroughly in cold water. Cook in a covered saucepan with no extra water until tender. Drain and chop.
2. Cook the noodles in boiling salted water until tender. Drain.
3. Brown the meat, chopped sausage and onion in the oil. Stir to break up the ground meat.
4. Add the tomatoes, tomato paste, salt and basil. Cover and cook over a low heat for ½ hour.
5. Stir the spinach into the meat sauce.
6. Put half the noodles into the buttered crockery pot.
7. Pour on half the meat sauce and sprinkle on half the Parmesan cheese. Cover with layers of remaining noodles, meat sauce and Parmesan cheese.
8. Spread the sour cream on the top.
9. Sprinkle on the grated cheddar cheese and chives.
10. Cover and cook on the high setting (300°F — 150°C) for about one hour.

Serves 6-8.

Simple Veal Stew

2 cloves garlic, minced
1 medium onion, chopped
3 tablespoons (45 g) butter
2 lb (1 kg) stewing veal, cubed
plain flour
salt and pepper
½ cup (125 ml) water

2½ tablespoons tomato paste
4 tablespoons red wine
  vinegar
½ teaspoon marjoram
2 teaspoons salt
chopped parsley

1. Saute the garlic and onion in half the butter in a large frypan until golden brown. Put into the crockery pot.
2. Coat the veal cubes in the flour seasoned with salt and pepper.
3. Melt the remaining butter in the same frypan and brown the meat. Put into the crockery pot.
4. Mix together the water, tomato paste, vinegar, marjoram and salt in the frypan. Scrape the bottom and cook over a low heat for one minute. Pour over the meat in the crockery pot and mix well.
5. Cover and cook on the low setting (200°F — 100°C) for about eight hours.
6. Serve sprinkled with parsley.

Serves 6.

Moroccan Veal Stew

4 tablespoons (60 g) butter
2 medium onions, chopped
2 teaspoons grated fresh
  ginger
2 teaspoons salt
1 teaspoon cumin
½ teaspoon black pepper

1 teaspoon cinnamon
2 cloves garlic, minced
2 lb (1 kg) stewing veal, cubed
1 cup dried apricots, chopped
½ cup raisins
1½ tablespoons honey
1½ tablespoons lemon juice

1. Melt the butter in a large frypan and saute the onions with the ginger, salt, cumin, pepper and cinnamon until the onions are golden brown.
2. Add the garlic and meat and cook until the meat is well browned, stirring frequently. Put into the crockery pot.
3. Stir the apricots and raisins into the meat mixture.
4. Cover and cook on the low setting (200°F — 100°C) for about eight hours.
5. Add the honey and lemon juice. Mix well. Turn the crockery pot to the high setting (300°F — 150°C) and cook for another 15 minutes.

Serves 6.

Spicy Frankfurters

1 cup (250 ml) tomato sauce
⅓ cup brown sugar
4 teaspoons malt vinegar
1 teaspoon Worcestershire
  sauce

2 teaspoons prepared
  mustard
1 clove garlic, minced
salt and pepper
1½ lb (750 g) frankfurters

1. Mix together the tomato sauce, brown sugar, vinegar, Worcestershire sauce, mustard, garlic and salt and pepper to taste.
2. Pour into the crockery pot and cook, covered, on the high setting (300°F — 150°C) for 15 minutes.
3. Add the frankfurters and cook until they are heated through.

Serves 4.

Veal Paprika

2 lb (1 kg) stewing veal, cut in
  cubes
¼ lb (125 g) bacon, chopped
1 medium onion, chopped
2 cloves garlic, minced
1½ teaspoons salt

¼ teaspoon black pepper
4 teaspoons paprika
2½ tablespoons plain flour
1 cup (250 ml) chicken stock
1 cup (250 g) sour cream
chopped parsley

1. Saute the veal and the bacon until the veal is browned.
2. Add the onion and garlic and saute until the onion is transparent.
3. Remove from the heat and stir in the salt, pepper, paprika and flour. Mix well.
4. Put into the crockery pot, cover and cook on the low setting (200°F — 100°C) for four to six hours or until the meat is tender.
5. Remove the meat from the crockery pot and keep warm.
6. Stir the sour cream into the liquid in the crockery pot. Heat through, then pour over the veal.
7. Garnish with chopped parsley.

Serves 4-6.

Stuffed Breast of Lamb

3 lb (1½ kg) breast of lamb
1½ teaspoons salt
water
⅓ cup (85 g) butter
½ lb (250 g) spinach
1 stalk celery, minced
1½ tablespoons chopped
    parsley

½ green pepper, minced
1 small onion minced
1 teaspoon salt
¼ teaspoon pepper
1½ cups dried bread crumbs
3 tablespoons (45 g) butter
salt and pepper

1. Put the breast of lamb into the crockery pot with the 1½ teaspoons salt and enough water to cover. Cover and cook on the low setting (200°F — 100°F) for six to eight hours.
2. Remove the lamb from the crockery pot and spread out on a cutting board. Remove the bones. Reserve one-third cup (85 ml) of the liquid from the crockery pot.
3. Melt half the butter in a large frypan and saute the spinach (which has been thoroughly washed, dried and chopped), celery, parsley, pepper and onion seasoned with the salt and pepper, for three minutes. Remove the vegetables to a large bowl.
4. Melt the other half of the butter and saute the bread crumbs for two minutes, stirring constantly. Add to the vegetables and mix well.
5. Spread the stuffing over the boned breast of lamb.
6. Place the roll in a buttered baking dish. Spread the three tablespoons of butter over the roll and season to taste with salt and pepper.
7. Bake in a 400°F (200°C) oven for about 20 minutes or until well-browned.

Serves 4-6.

Stuffed Breast of Veal

4 tablespoons (60 g) butter	2 lb (1 kg) boned veal breast
2 medium onions, minced	¼ cup (65 ml) vegetable oil
2 cups fresh bread crumbs	¼ cup (65 ml) water
1½ teaspoons salt	1 bay leaf
¼ teaspoon pepper	1 small onion, peeled
1½ teaspoons sage	4 whole cloves
5½ tablespoons chopped parsley	1 carrot, quartered
	¼ teaspoon thyme

1. Melt the butter in a large frypan and saute the onions until transparent.
2. Add the bread crumbs, salt, pepper, sage and parsley and mix well.
3. Spread the bread crumb mixture over the boned breast of veal.
4. Roll up and secure with skewers or toothpicks.
5. Heat the oil in the same frypan and brown the roll on all sides. Put into the crockery pot.
6. Pour the water into the frypan and scrape the bottom. Pour over the meat.
7. Put bay leaf, onion stuck with cloves, carrot and thyme in the crockery pot.
8. Cover and cook on the low setting (200°F — 100°C) for four to six hours. Remove bay leaf, onion and carrot before serving.

Serves 4-6.

Pork and Beans

4 pork chops	¼ cup chilli sauce
4 teaspoons oil	1½ teaspoons brown sugar
salt and pepper	1 teaspoon prepared mustard
1 clove garlic, minced	1 cup canned kidney beans
2 medium onions, chopped	1 cup canned lima beans

1. Brown the chops on both sides in the oil in a frypan. Season to taste with salt and pepper and put into the crockery pot.
2. Saute the garlic and onions in the frypan until the onions are transparent. Put over the chops.
3. Remove frypan from the heat and stir in the chilli sauce, scraping the bottom of the frypan.
4. Add the brown sugar and mustard and mix well. Pour over the meat.
5. Cover and cook on the low setting (200°F — 100°C) for six to eight hours.
6. Add the kidney and lima beans. Mix well, cook for another 1½ hours.

Serves 4.

Veal Pot Roast

4 lb (2 kg) rump of veal	4 stalks celery, cut in chunks
2½ tablespoons oil	¼ cup (65 ml) water
salt and pepper	3 tablespoons (45 g) butter
3 carrots, sliced	2½ tablespoons plain flour
2 medium onions, quartered	⅓ cup (85 ml) white wine

1. Brown the veal on all sides in the oil in a frypan. Season to taste with salt and pepper.
2. Put the vegetables into the crockery pot and place the meat on top.
3. Pour the water into the frypan and scrape the bottom. Cook over a low heat for one minute, then pour onto the meat.
4. Cover and cook on the low setting (200°F — 100°C) for five to seven hours.
5. Remove the meat and the vegetables from the crockery pot and keep warm.
6. Melt the butter in a saucepan and stir in the flour. Cook over a low heat for 30 seconds.
7. Add the liquid from the crockery pot and, stirring constantly, cook until thick and smooth.
8. Add the wine and cook for another two minutes. Season to taste with salt and pepper. Pour over the meat.

Serves 8-10.

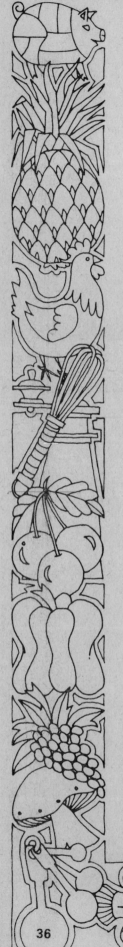

Chili Con Carne

1 lb (500 g) ground beef
2 medium onions, chopped
2 cloves garlic, minced
1 teaspoon oregano
½ teaspoon salt
1 teaspoon cumin

chili powder to taste
½ teaspoon salt
250 g (½ lb) ripe tomatoes
⅔ cup (165 ml) tomato puree
2 cups canned kidney beans
4 cups hot cooked rice

1. Brown the meat in a frypan stirring with a fork to break it up.
2. Put the meat in the crockery pot with all the remaining ingredients except the rice. Mix well.
3. Cover and cook on the low setting (200°F — 100°C) for five to seven hours.
4. Serve over the hot rice.

Serves 6.

Pork with Pears

2 lb (1 kg) boneless pork loin roast
1 teaspoon salt
¼ teaspoon pepper
¼ teaspoon dried dill
¼ teaspoon rosemary
½ lb (250 g) potatoes, peeled and diced

6 firm pears, peeled and halved
4 teaspoons caraway seeds
4 teaspoons Worcestershire sauce
½ cup (125 ml) beef stock
2½ tablespoons cornstarch
4 tablespoons cold water

1. Sprinkle the salt, pepper, dill and rosemary on the pork.
2. Put the potatoes into the crockery pot and place the seasoned pork on top of them.
3. Put the pear halves on top of the pork and sprinkle with the caraway seeds.
4. Mix together the Worcestershire sauce and the beef stock and pour over the pears.
5. Cover and cook on the low setting (200°F — 100°C) for eight to ten hours.
6. Remove the meat and pears to a serving dish and keep warm.
7. Mix together the cornstarch and cold water and stir into the liquid in the crockery pot until smooth and thick. Pour over the meat and pears.

Serves 4-6.

Cabanossi Stuffed Meat Loaf

1 lb (500 g) cabanossi sausage
2 eggs
½ cup (125 ml) milk
2 slices brown bread, crust removed
1½ teaspoons salt
2 teaspoons Worcestershire sauce

1 beef stock cube
1 medium onion, quartered
1½ lb (750 g) ground beef
¼ cup (65 ml) tomato sauce
1 teaspoon French mustard
2½ tablespoons brown sugar

1. Put the sausages in a saucepan with enough water to cover. Bring to a boil and cook for ten minutes. Drain.

2. Mix together the eggs, milk, bread, salt, Worcestershire sauce, stock cube and onion. Put into an electric blender and whirl for 30 seconds or until smooth. (As an alternative, you may put the ingredients through any kind of food mill.)

3. Mix the meat with the pureed mixture.

4. Divide the meat mixture in half and press one half on the bottom of the crockery pot.

5. Lay the drained sausages on top, then cover with the remaining meat mixture.

6. Mix together the tomato sauce, mustard and brown sugar. Spread over the meat loaf.

7. Cover and cook on the high setting (300°F — 150°C) for about one hour. Reduce the heat to the low setting (200°F — 100°C) and cook for another five hours.

Serves 6.

Bean Pot Beef Stew

2½ tablespoons oil	½ cup oatmeal
1 medium onion, chopped	4 medium potatoes, quartered
1 lb (500 g) round steak, cut into cubes	1 cup (250 ml) water
2 medium carrots, diced	1 teaspoon salt
1 turnip, diced	¼ teaspoon pepper
1 cup dried lima beans	

1. Heat the oil in a large frypan and saute the onion until transparent.
2. Add the meat, carrots and turnip and cook over a medium heat until the meat is browned on all sides.
3. Put the lima beans into the crockery pot.
4. Pour the meat and vegetables over the lima beans.
5. Sprinkle on the oatmeal.
6. Press the potatoes down into the stew and pour on the water.
7. Sprinkle on the salt and pepper.
8. Cover and cook on the low setting (200°F — 100°C) for six to eight hours.

Serves 4.

Meat Loaf

½ cup (125 ml) milk	1 small onion, minced
2 slices bread	1½ teaspoons salt
1½ lb (750 g) ground beef	½ teaspoon pepper
2 eggs	1½ teaspoons dry mustard
2½ tablespoons tomato paste	1 can (12 oz) tomatoes

1. Pour the milk over the bread on a large plate and allow to stand until the bread has absorbed all the milk. Break the bread up with a fork.
2. Thoroughly mix together the bread and the meat.
3. Beat the eggs with the tomato paste and add to the meat. Mix well.
4. Blend in the onion, salt, pepper and mustard.
5. Form the meat mixture into a round loaf and put into the crockery pot.
6. Pour the tomatoes with the liquid over the meat loaf.
7. Cover and cook on the low setting (200°F — 100°C) for five to seven hours.
8. Turn the crockery pot to the high setting (300°F — 150°C) and cook, uncovered, until the liquid is slightly reduced.

Serves 4-6.

Italian Beef Stew

3 lb (1½ kg) chuck steak, cut into cubes
4 tablespoons bacon fat or oil
2 medium onions, sliced
2 cloves garlic, minced
1 lb (500 g) tomatoes, chopped
½ cup (125 ml) red wine
1½ teaspoons salt
½ teaspoon basil

¼ teaspoon oregano
¼ teaspoon black pepper
5 medium carrots, sliced
½ lb (250 g) small onions, peeled and left whole
2 green peppers, cut in large slices
2½ tablespoons plain flour
grated Parmesan cheese

1. In a large frypan brown the meat in the bacon fat or oil.
2. Add the onions and garlic and cook until the onions are golden brown.
3. Add the tomatoes and cook for another five minutes. Put into the crockery pot.
4. Pour the wine in the frypan with the salt, basil, oregano and black pepper. Scrape the bottom of the frypan and cook over a low heat for one minute. Pour over the meat in the crockery pot.
5. Add the carrots, onions and green peppers and mix well.
6. Cover and cook on the low setting (200°F — 100°C) for eight to ten hours. Skim off any fat.
7. When the meat is cooked, spoon out two tablespoons of the liquid from the crockery pot into a small saucepan. Mix in the flour until smooth.
8. Slowly add about one cup of the liquid and, stirring constantly, cook until thick and smooth. Pour into the crockery pot.
9. Turn the crockery pot to the high setting (300°F — 150°C) and simmer for five minutes.
10. Serve sprinkled with Parmesan cheese.

Serves 8.

Three-Meat Stew

¼ lb (125 g) bacon, chopped
½ lb (250 g) pork, cut in cubes
½ lb (250 g) beef, cut in cubes
½ lb (250 g) lamb, cut in cubes
4 medium carrots, sliced
3 medium onions, sliced
3 medium potatoes, sliced
2½ tablespoons chopped
   parsley

4 teaspoons tomato paste
½ cup (125 ml) beef stock
1 teaspoon salt
¼ teaspoon pepper
½ teaspoon marjoram
¼ teaspoon thyme

1. Cook the bacon in a large frypan over a medium heat until half cooked.
2. Add the meat and brown on all sides. Put into the crockery pot.
3. Put the vegetables and parsley into the frypan and saute until the onions are transparent. Put into the crockery pot.
4. Mix together the tomato paste and the beef stock in the frypan. Scrape the bottom. Add the salt, pepper, marjoram and thyme and cook over a low heat for one minute.
5. Pour into the crockery pot with the meat and vegetables. Mix well.
6. Cover and cook on the low setting (200°F — 100°C) for six to eight hours.

Serves 6.

Hungarian Goulash

4 tablespoons (60 g) butter
3 cups thinly sliced onions
4 medium potatoes,
   quartered
1½ lb (750 g) chuck steak, cut
   into large cubes

2½ teaspoons salt
4 teaspoons paprika
1 cup (250 ml) water

1. Melt two tablespoons of the butter in a large frypan. Saute the onions until golden brown. Remove to the crockery pot.
2. Put the potatoes on top of the onions.
3. Melt the remaining butter in the frypan and brown the meat on all sides.
4. Sprinkle the meat with the salt and paprika and put into the crockery pot.
5. Pour the water into the frypan and scrape the bottom. Cook on a low heat for one minute. Pour over the meat.
6. Cover and cook on the low setting (200°F — 100°C) for eight to ten hours.

Serves 4.

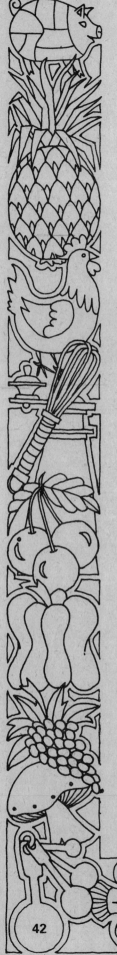

Beef Stew

⅓ cup plain flour
½ teaspoon black pepper
1 teaspoon salt
2 lb (1 kg) chuck steak, cut into large cubes
4 tablespoons oil
2 medium onions, chopped
3 cloves garlic, minced
1 green pepper, chopped
1¾ cups (435 ml) water

4 tablespoons tomato paste
½ teaspoon salt
2 teaspoons Worcestershire sauce
4 medium carrots, sliced
4 medium potatoes, quartered
4 tablespoons chopped parsley

1. Mix together the flour, pepper and salt.
2. Coat the cubes of meat thoroughly in the flour and brown in the oil in a large frypan. As each piece browns, remove from the frypan and put into the crockery pot.
3. Saute the onions, garlic and green pepper in the frypan until the onions are golden brown. Remove from the heat.
4. Stir the remaining flour into the frypan, then add the water and stir until smooth.
5. Add the tomato paste, salt and Worcestershire sauce. Mix thoroughly, scraping the bottom of the frypan. Pour into the crockery pot.
6. Put the carrots and potatoes on top of the meat.
7. Cover and cook on the low setting (200°F — 100°C) for eight to ten hours.
8. Serve garnished with chopped parsley.

Serves 6.

Veal Stew with Wine

2 lb (1 kg) stewing veal, cubed
plain flour
salt and pepper
4 tablespoons (60 g) butter
1 cup (250 ml) white wine
1 cup (250 ml) beef stock
1½ teaspoons salt

1 small onion, chopped
2 cloves garlic, minced
1 teaspoon tarragon
1 teaspoon grated lemon rind
¼ cup (65 g) sour cream
2 teaspoons lemon juice

CONTINUED ON NEXT PAGE

1. Coat the veal cubes with the flour seasoned with salt and pepper.
2. Melt the butter in a large frypan and thoroughly brown the meat. Put the meat into the crockery pot.
3. Pour the wine and beef stock into the frypan with the salt. Mix well and scrape the bottom of the frypan. Cook over a low heat for two minutes. Pour over the meat in the crockery pot.
4. Add the onion, garlic, tarragon and grated lemon rind and mix well.
5. Cover and cook on the low setting (200°F — 100°C) for eight hours.
6. Remove the meat from the crockery pot and keep warm.
7. Turn the crockery pot to the high setting (300°F — 150°C) and cook the sauce, uncovered, until reduced and thickened.
8. Stir in the sour cream and lemon juice.
9. Return the meat to the crockery pot and heat thoroughly.

Serves 6.

Lamb Shank Stew

4 lamb shanks
salt and pepper
1 teaspoon grated lemon rind
1 teaspoon basil
2 cloves garlic, minced
1 medium onion, chopped
3 tablespoons (45 g) butter

4 tablespoons chopped parsley
1 medium carrot, chopped
½ cup (125 ml) red wine
½ cup (125 ml) beef stock
salt and pepper

1. Rub the lamb shanks with salt and pepper to taste, the grated lemon rind and the basil. Put into the crockery pot.
2. Saute the garlic and onion in the butter until the onion is transparent.
3. Add the parsley and carrot and cook for another three minutes. Put into the crockery pot.
4. Mix together the red wine and beef stock in the frypan, scraping the bottom. Season to taste with salt and pepper. Pour over the lamb shanks.
5. Cover and cook on the low setting (200°F — 100°C) for eight hours.

Serves 4.

Beef Stew with Zucchini

2 lb (1 kg) chuck steak, cut into cubes
2½ tablespoons oil
2 teaspoons salt
½ teaspoon black pepper
2 medium onions, chopped
½ cup (125 ml) water
¼ teaspoon oregano

1 medium green pepper, sliced
1 bay leaf
2 stalks celery, sliced
5 medium potatoes, quartered
1 lb (500 g) zucchini, sliced
2½ tablespoons plain flour

1. Brown the meat in the oil in a large frypan. Sprinkle on half the salt and pepper and put into the crockery pot.
2. Saute the onions in the same frypan until golden brown. Put into the crockery pot.
3. Pour the water into the frypan and scrape the bottom.
4. Add the remaining salt and pepper, oregano, green pepper, bay leaf and celery. Mix well, then put into the crockery pot.
5. Add the potatoes and zucchini to the crockery pot and stir well.
6. Cover and cook on the low setting (200°F — 100°C) for eight to ten hours.
7. When the meat is cooked, skim 2½ tablespoons of the fat from the cooking liquid and mix with the flour in a small saucepan. Pour the rest of the liquid into the saucepan and cook, stirring constantly, until smooth and thick. Return to the stew and mix thoroughly.

Serves 4-6.

Paprika Beef

1½ lb (750 g) round steak, cut into cubes
4 tablespoons oil
1 teaspoon paprika
2 medium onions, sliced
2 teaspoons salt
1½ cups (375 ml) water

2 tablespoons brown sugar
2 bay leaves
4 tablespoons plain flour
½ cup (125 ml) water
chopped parsley

1. Brown the meat in a large frypan in the oil and paprika.
2. Add the onions and cook until the onions are browned. Put the meat and the onions in the crockery pot.
3. Blend the salt, water, sugar and bay leaves in the frypan. Scrape the bottom of the frypan and cook for two minutes. Pour into the crockery pot.
4. Cover and cook on the low setting (200°F — 100°C) for eight to ten hours.
5. Mix the plain flour with the water.
6. Pour the liquid from the crockery pot into a saucepan.
7. Add the flour mixture and, stirring constantly, cook over a medium heat until thick and smooth. Return to the crockery pot and mix thoroughly. Heat through and serve with chopped parsley sprinkled on top.

Serves 4-6.

Corned Beef Boiled Dinner

4 lb (2 kg) corned beef
water to cover
6 small white onions, peeled
1 onion, peeled, stuck with 8 cloves
2 bay leaves
½ teaspoon thyme
2 teaspoons salt
3 parsnips, peeled

8 medium carrots, halved
1 turnip, cut in chunks
5 medium potatoes, quartered
3 stalks celery, cut in 3-inch (8-cm) lengths
2½ tablespoons chopped parsley

1. Place all the ingredients except the parsley in the crockery pot.
2. Cover and cook on the low setting (200°F — 100°C) for ten to twelve hours.
3. To serve, drain and place the corned beef on a serving platter with the vegetables around it.
4. Sprinkle with chopped parsley.

Serves 10.

Lamb Meat Loaf

¼ cup (65 g) butter
½ lb (250 g) mushrooms, chopped
1 small onion, chopped
2½ tablespoons minced parsley
2 slices bread
½ cup (125 ml) milk

2 lb (1 kg) ground lamb
1½ teaspoons salt
¼ teaspoon pepper
1 teaspoon rosemary
2½ tablespoons lemon juice
1 egg

1. Saute the mushrooms, onion and parsley in the butter in a large frypan for about seven minutes. Remove the frypan from the heat.
2. Pour the milk over the bread and allow to stand until the milk has been completely absorbed, then break up the bread.
3. In a large bowl, mix together the meat, soaked bread, the mushroom mixture, salt, pepper, rosemary and lemon juice.
4. Add the slightly beaten egg and mix thoroughly.
5. Shape the mixture into a round loaf and put into the lightly buttered crockery pot.
6. Cover and cook on the low setting (200°F — 100°C) for five to seven hours.
7. Serve with the cooking juices poured over the loaf.

Serves 4-6.

Orange Pork Chops

4 thick pork chops
salt and pepper
2 tablespoons (30 g) butter
½ cup (125 ml) orange juice
⅓ cup (85 ml) tomato sauce
2½ tablespoons orange
   marmalade

1 teaspoon grated orange
  rind
½ teaspoon grated lemon rind
orange slices
chopped chives

1. Rub the pork chops with salt and pepper and brown on both sides in the butter. Put into the crockery pot.
2. Mix together the orange juice, tomato sauce, marmalade, orange rind and lemon rind in the frypan. Scrape the bottom of the pan and cook over a low heat for two minutes. Pour over the pork chops.
3. Cover and cook on the low setting (200°F — 100°C) for eight hours.
4. Serve the chops with the sauce poured over them and topped with orange slices and chopped chives.

Serves 4.

Topside Roast with Sour Cream Sauce

1 teaspoon salt
4 lb (2 kg) corner topside
3 tablespoons (45 g) butter
1 medium onion, sliced
1 cup (250 ml) red wine

1 teaspoon salt
½ teaspoon black pepper
2½ tablespoons plain flour
⅔ cup (165 g) sour cream

1. Rub the salt on the corner topside.
2. Melt the butter in a large frypan and brown the meat on all sides. Put into the crockery pot.
3. Saute the onion in the same frypan until golden brown.
4. Add the wine and scrape the bottom of the frypan.
5. Add the salt and pepper and pour over the meat.
6. Cover and cook on the low setting (200°F — 100°C) for about ten hours.
7. Take about two tablespoons of the liquid from the crockery pot and mix with the flour in a small saucepan.
8. Add the rest of the liquid and cook, stirring constantly, until smooth and thick.
9. Remove from heat and stir in the sour cream. Pour the sauce over the meat and serve immediately.

Serves 8.

Tongue with Port Sauce

1 beef tongue
3 teaspoons salt
2 cups (500 ml) water
1 bay leaf
1 medium onion, sliced
1 carrot, cut into large chunks
10 whole peppercorns

4 teaspoons lemon juice
1 cup (250 ml) beef stock
2 tablespoons cornstarch
2½ tablespoons water
salt and pepper

Port Sauce:
½ cup (125 ml) port
1½ tablespoons blackcurrant
   jam

1. Rinse the tongue in cold water and put into the crockery pot with the salt, water, bay leaf, onion, carrot and peppercorns.
2. Cover and cook on the low setting (200°F — 100°C) for eight hours.
3. Remove the tongue from the stock and when slightly cool, skin with a sharp knife. Slice and keep warm while making the sauce.
4. Mix together the port, blackcurrant jam, lemon juice and beef stock in a small saucepan. Heat gently.
5. Mix the cornstarch with the water and add to the port mixture, stirring constantly. Cook until thickened. Season to taste with salt and pepper.
6. Pour the sauce over the sliced tongue and serve immediately.

Serves 8.

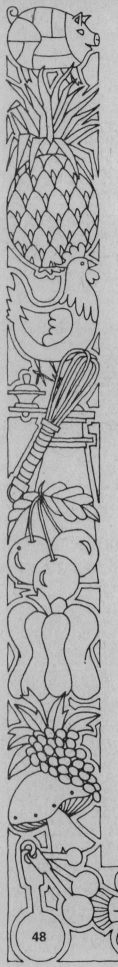

Lamb Meat Balls

2 lb (1 kg) ground lamb
½ cup mashed potatoes
2 eggs, slightly beaten
½ cup pine nuts
4 tablespoons raisins, chopped
2 tablespoons minced parsley
¼ teaspoon nutmeg
2 cloves garlic, minced

1½ teaspoons salt
½ teaspoon black pepper
4 tablespoons (60 g) butter
1 medium onion, chopped
½ lb (250 g) tomatoes, chopped
½ cup (125 ml) beef stock
1½ tablespoons tomato paste
¼ cup (65 ml) red wine

1. Mix together the lamb, potatoes, eggs, pine nuts, raisins, parsley, nutmeg, garlic, salt and pepper. Form into small balls.
2. Melt half the butter in a large frypan and brown the meat balls. Put into the crockery pot.
3. Melt the remaining butter in the frypan and saute the onion until transparent.
4. Add tomatoes, beef stock, tomato paste and red wine. Mix and scrape the bottom of pan. Cook on a low heat for two minutes. Pour over the meat balls.
5. Cover and cook on the low setting (200°F — 100°C) for about two hours.

Serves 4-6.

Lamb Chops with Prunes

2 medium onions, chopped
3 tablespoons (45 g) butter
8 lamb chops
salt and pepper
2 teaspoons grated fresh ginger
½ teaspoon cumin

2 cloves garlic, minced
1 teaspoon cinnamon
¼ teaspoon nutmeg
1 cup prunes, stoned
4 tablespoons honey
2½ tablespoons lemon juice

1. Saute the onions in the butter in a large frypan until transparent.
2. Add the chops and brown well on both sides.
3. Add salt and pepper to taste, ginger, cumin, garlic, cinnamon and nutmeg. Cook for two minutes. Put into the crockery pot.
4. Put the prunes on top of the chops.
5. Cover and cook on the low setting (200°F — 100°C) for six hours.
6. Just before serving, remove the chops and stir in the honey and lemon juice. Pour over the chops and serve.

Serves 4.

Meat and Bean Stew

1½ cups dried haricot beans	4 tablespoons tomato paste
4 cups (1 quart) water	½ cup (125 ml) beef stock
¼ lb (125 g) bacon, chopped	1 medium carrot, grated
3 medium onions, chopped	2 cloves garlic, minced
1 lb (500 g) cubed lamb	1 teaspoon marjoram
1 lb (500 g) cubed pork	salt and pepper
1 cup (250 ml) white wine	1 lb (500 g) Italian sausage

1. Soak the beans overnight in enough water to cover. Drain. Simmer the beans in the 4 cups of water for one hour. Drain. Put into the crockery pot.
2. Cook the bacon in a frypan for three minutes.
3. Add the onions and cook until they are golden brown. Put into the crockery pot.
4. Brown the lamb and pork in the same frypan in the remaining bacon dripping. When brown, put into the crockery pot.
5. Mix together the wine, tomato paste and stock in the frypan. Scrape the bottom of the pan and cook over a low heat for two minutes. Pour into the crockery pot.
6. Stir in the carrot, garlic, marjoram and salt and pepper to taste.
7. Cover and cook on the low setting (200°F — 100°C) for eight hours.
8. Slice the sausage, lay on the top and cook for another hour.

Serves 8.

Lamb Curry

2 lb (1 kg) stewing lamb, cubed
2½ tablespoons oil
4 teaspoons curry powder
2 medium onions, chopped
2 cooking apples, peeled and diced
2 teaspoons grated fresh ginger
3 cloves garlic, minced
2½ tablespoons plain flour
1 cup (250 ml) beef stock
1 cup (250 ml) red wine
1½ tablespoons lemon juice
1½ teaspoons salt
½ teaspoon pepper
hot rice

1. Brown the meat in the oil in a large frypan. Put the browned meat into the crockery pot.
2. Saute the curry powder and onions in the same frypan until the onions are transparent.
3. Add the apples, ginger, garlic and flour and cook until glazed. Put into the crockery pot.
4. Mix together the beef stock, wine, lemon juice, salt and pepper in the frypan. Scrape the bottom of the pan and cook over a low heat for two minutes. Pour over the meat and mix well.
5. Cover and cook on the low setting (200°F — 100°C) for 8-10 hours.
6. Serve the curry on top of hot rice.

Serves 6.

New England Corned Beef

4 lb (2 kg) corned beef
water to cover
2 bay leaves
1 teaspoon thyme
1 medium onion, peeled
1½ tablespoons chopped parsley
10 cloves
⅔ cup (165 ml) maple syrup

1. Put the beef, water, bay leaves, thyme, onion and parsley in the crockery pot.
2. Cover and cook on the low setting (200°F — 100°C) for ten to twelve hours.
3. Remove the meat from the crockery pot and stick with the cloves.
4. Put on a meat rack in a shallow baking dish and pour the syrup over the meat.
5. Bake in a 350°F (180°C) oven for about ½ hour basting frequently with the syrup.

Serves 8.

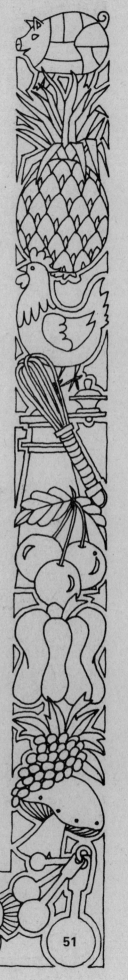

Rabbit Chasseur

3 lb (1½ kg) rabbit pieces
1½ teaspoons salt
½ teaspoon pepper
4 tablespoons oil
2 medium onions, chopped
2 medium green peppers,
   chopped
4 medium tomatoes, chopped

3 cloves garlic, minced
1 cup (250 ml) red wine
½ teaspoon thyme
¼ teaspoon marjoram
½ lb (250 g) mushrooms,
   sliced
½ teaspoon salt
chopped chives

1. Sprinkle the rabbit pieces with the salt and pepper and brown well in the oil in a large frypan. Remove from the frypan and keep warm.
2. Saute the onions, green peppers, tomatoes and garlic in the frypan until the onions are browned.
3. Put the vegetables into the crockery pot and place the rabbit pieces on top.
4. Pour the wine into the frypan with the thyme and marjoram. Cook over a low heat for one minute, scraping the bottom of the frypan. Pour over the rabbit.
5. Cover and cook on the low setting (200°F — 100°C) for five to seven hours.
6. Skim a little of the fat from the crockery pot and saute the mushrooms for ten minutes with the ½ teaspoon salt. Stir into the crockery pot. Heat through and serve sprinkled with chopped chives.

Serves 4-6.

Chicken

Chicken with Vegetables

1 chicken (3 lb - 1½ kg)
salt and pepper
3 tablespoons (45 g) butter
2 medium carrots, sliced
2 parsnips, sliced
1 green pepper, chopped
2 medium tomatoes,
   quartered

2 stalks celery, sliced
1 medium onion, chopped
2 cloves garlic, minced
½ teaspoon thyme
2 cups (500 ml) chicken stock
1 cup (250 ml) white wine

1. Season the chicken with salt and pepper and brown in the butter in a large frypan on all sides. Remove to the crockery pot.
2. Pour a little water into the frypan and scrape the bottom. Pour the water and scrapings over the chicken.
3. Sprinkle all the vegetables around the chicken.
4. Mix the garlic with the thyme, chicken stock and white wine and pour over the chicken.
5. Cover and cook on the low setting (200°F — 100°C) for about eight hours. Remove the chicken and vegetables and keep warm.
6. Skim the fat from the liquid. Turn the heat up to the high setting (300°F — 150°C) and boil rapidly until it is reduced to one cup. Pour over the carved chicken and vegetables.

Serves 4.

Poached Chicken

3 lb (1½ kg) chicken pieces
2½ tablespoons plain flour
1½ teaspoons salt
¼ teaspoon pepper
¼ lb (125 g) bacon, chopped
1 medium onion, chopped
1 stalk celery, sliced
1 medium carrot, chopped

3 medium cooking apples, diced
6 peppercorns
1 bay leaf
¼ teaspoon thyme
½ cup (125 ml) rose wine
chopped parsley

1. Coat the chicken with the flour seasoned with salt and pepper.
2. Saute the bacon in a large frypan until crisp.
3. Add the vegetables and apples and saute until the onion is transparent. Put into the crockery pot.
4. Mix the peppercorns, bay leaf and thyme into the vegetables and apples.
5. Place the chicken on top and pour the wine over all.
6. Cover and cook on the low setting (200°F — 100°C) for five to seven hours.
7. Serve garnished with chopped parsley. Serves 4-6.

Red Chicken

2 tablespoons oil
1 chicken (3 lb - 1½ kg)
4 medium onions, chopped
6 medium tomatoes, chopped
1 orange, sliced, unpeeled
1½ teaspoons brown sugar

1½ teaspoons salt
¼ teaspoon pepper
½ cup (125 ml) chicken stock
⅓ cup raspberry jam
⅓ cup (85 ml) sherry

1. Brown the chicken in the oil in a large frypan on all sides. Remove and keep warm.
2. Saute the onions in the frypan until golden brown. Put into the crockery pot.
3. Add the tomatoes, orange, sugar, salt and pepper to the onions.
4. Put the chicken into the crockery pot on top of the tomato mixture.
5. Pour the chicken stock into the frypan and scrape the bottom. Cook over a low heat for one minute and pour over the chicken.
6. Cover and cook on the low setting (200°F — 100°C) for five to seven hours. When the chicken is cooked, remove from the crockery pot and keep warm.
7. Pour the liquid from the crockery pot into a saucepan. Boil rapidly to reduce to a thick sauce.
8. Add the jam and the sherry and bring back to the boil, stirring constantly.
9. Pour the sauce over the chicken and serve immediately. Serves 4-6.

Chicken Provencal

½ lb (250 g) bacon, chopped
3 tablespoons (45 g) butter
2 medium carrots, grated
2 medium onions, chopped
3 lb (1½ kg) chicken pieces
¼ cup (65 ml) brandy
3 medium tomatoes, chopped

⅔ cup (165 ml) red wine
¼ teaspoon marjoram
¼ teaspoon basil
2½ tablespoons chopped
   parsley
salt and pepper

1. Cook bacon in a large frypan until crisp. Remove bacon to the crockery pot.
2. Add the butter to the bacon fat and saute the carrots and onions until soft. Put the carrots and onions into the crockery pot.
3. Brown the chicken pieces on all sides in the frypan.
4. Pour the brandy on the chicken and ignite. When the flames go out, put the chicken in the crockery pot.
5. Add the tomatoes, wine, marjoram, basil, parsley and salt and pepper to taste to the chicken.
6. Cover and cook on the low setting (200°F — 100°C) for six hours.
7. Remove the chicken, skim the fat from the sauce and pour over the chicken. Serve immediately.

Serves 4.

Chicken with Pineapple

2 medium onions, chopped
5 tablespoons (75 g) butter
6 chicken breasts, halved
plain flour

salt and pepper
1 can (1 lb) pineapple slices
hot cooked rice
chopped parsley

1. Saute the onions in one tablespoon of butter in a fry pan until transparent. Put into the crockery pot.
2. Coat the chicken pieces with flour seasoned with salt and pepper.
3. Melt two tablespoons of the butter and brown the chicken on both sides. Put into the crockery pot.
4. Pour the juice from the pineapple over the chicken.
5. Cover and cook on the low setting (200°F — 100°C) for four hours.
6. Melt the remaining butter and saute the pineapple slices until golden brown.
7. Serve the chicken on top of the rice and topped with pineapple slices and chopped parsley.

Serves 6.

Coq Au Vin

3 spring onions, chopped (white part only)
½ lb (250 g) bacon, chopped
1 chicken (3 lb - 1½ kg)
salt and pepper
thyme
8 small onions, whole
1 cup (250 ml) red wine

1 cup (250 ml) chicken stock
2 cloves garlic, minced
½ lb (250 g) mushrooms, sliced
3 tablespoons (45 g) butter
4 teaspoons cornstarch
2½ tablespoons cold water
chopped parsley

1. Saute the chopped onions and bacon in a large frypan until the bacon is crisp. Remove the bacon and onion and put into the crockery pot.
2. Season the chicken with salt, pepper and thyme and brown on all sides in the bacon fat. Put into the crockery pot.
3. Peel the whole onions and brown in the bacon fat. Put into the crockery pot with the chicken.
4. Pour the wine and the chicken stock with the garlic into the fry pan and scrape the bottom of any bits. Pour over the chicken.
5. Cover the crockery pot and cook on the low setting (200°F — 100°C) for eight hours.
6. Saute the mushrooms in the butter and add to the chicken. Turn the crockery pot to the high setting (300°F — 150°C) and bring to a boil. Remove chicken.
7. Blend together the cornstarch and water and add to the crockery pot. Stir until thickened.
8. Pour the sauce over the chicken and sprinkle with chopped parsley.

Serves 4.

Orange Chicken

3 lb (1½ kg) chicken pieces
3 tablespoons (45 g) butter
1 carrot, chopped
1 medium onion, chopped
1½ tablespoons chopped parsley
1 cup (250 ml) chicken stock

salt and pepper
4 tablespoons orange juice concentrate
4 tablespoons currant jam
orange slices
chopped parsley

CONTINUED ON NEXT PAGE

1. Saute the chicken pieces in the butter in a large frypan until well browned.
2. Add the carrot, onion and parsley and cook until the onion is transparent. Put into the crockery pot.
3. Pour the chicken stock into the frypan and season to taste with salt and pepper. Scrape all the bits off the bottom and cook over a low heat for two minutes. Pour over the chicken.
4. Cover and cook on the low setting (200°F — 100°C) for six hours. Remove the chicken pieces from the crockery pot and keep warm.
5. Strain the liquid, skim the fat and return to the crockery pot. Turn the heat up to the high setting (300°F — 150°C) and boil rapidly until the liquid is reduced to about one cup.
6. Add the orange juice concentrate and currant jam. Mix well and heat thoroughly. Pour over the chicken and serve immediately, garnished with orange slices and parsley.

Chicken Curry

1 chicken (3 lb - 1½ kg)
2 cups (500 ml) chicken stock
1 large cooking apple, peeled and cubed
2 cloves garlic, minced
1 medium onion, chopped
3 stalks celery, sliced
4 teaspoons curry powder or to taste
4 tablespoons (60 g) butter
salt and pepper
hot cooked rice

1. Put the chicken in the crockery pot with the chicken stock.
2. Cover and cook on the low setting (200°F — 100°C) for eight hours. Remove from the stock and cool.
3. When the chicken is cool, remove the meat from the skin and bones and cut into small pieces.
4. Saute the apple, garlic, onion, celery and curry powder in the butter for five minutes.
5. Add the chicken and one cup of the chicken stock.
6. Season to taste with salt and pepper and heat thoroughly.
7. Serve over hot cooked rice.

Chicken with Grapes

3 lb (1½ kg) chicken pieces
3 tablespoons (45 g) butter
1 medium carrot, chopped
1 medium onion, chopped
⅔ cup (165 ml) white wine
½ cup (125 ml) chicken stock

salt and pepper
5 tablespoons orange
   marmalade
2 tablespoons lemon juice
½ lb (250 g) seedless grapes

1. Saute the chicken pieces in the butter in a frypan until well browned.
2. Add the carrot and onion and cook until the onion is transparent.
3. Put the chicken and vegetables into the crockery pot.
4. Pour the wine, chicken stock and salt and pepper to taste into the frypan. Scrape the bottom and cook over a low heat for two minutes. Pour over the chicken.
5. Cover and cook on the low setting (200°F — 100°C) for six hours. Remove the chicken from the crockery pot and keep warm.
6. Strain the liquid in the crockery pot and pour into a saucepan. Discard the carrot and onion.
7. Skim the fat from the liquid and boil rapidly until it is reduced to one cup.
8. Add the marmalade, lemon juice and grapes and heat thoroughly.
9. Pour the sauce over the chicken and serve immediately.

Serves 4.

Chicken with Brandy

3 lb (1½ kg) chicken pieces
3 tablespoons (45 g) butter
salt
4 tablespoons brandy
½ cup (125 ml) chicken stock
2½ tablespoons chopped
    parsley

¼ teaspoon marjoram
¼ teaspoon thyme
⅔ cup (165 ml) white wine
4 teaspoons cornstarch
2½ tablespoons water
⅓ cup (85 ml) cream

1. Saute the chicken pieces on all sides in a frypan until well browned. Season to taste with salt.
2. Pour the brandy over the chicken and ignite. When flames have gone out, put the chicken pieces with the pan juices into the crockery pot.
3. Mix together the chicken stock, parsley, marjoram, thyme and white wine in the frypan. Scrape the bottom and cook for one minute. Pour over the chicken.
4. Cover and cook for six hours on the low setting (200°F — 100°C). Remove the chicken and keep warm.
5. Mix together the cornstarch and water and add to the crockery pot. Turn onto the high setting (300°F — 150°C) and cook, stirring constantly until thick.
6. Turn off the heat and stir in the cream. Pour over the chicken pieces and serve immediately.

Serves 4.

Stuffed Chicken

1 chicken (3 lb - 1½ kg)
3 tablespoons (45 g) butter
1½ cups cooked rice
¼ cup slivered almonds

salt and pepper
¼ cup raisins
1 teaspoon grated lemon rind
⅔ cup (165 ml) white wine

1. Brown the chicken on all sides in the butter in a large frypan.
2. Mix together the rice, almonds, salt and pepper to taste and the raisins.
3. Sprinkle the lemon rind into the cavity of the chicken, then stuff with the rice mixture. Close cavity with a skewer.
4. Put the chicken in the crockery pot and pour the wine over it.
5. Cover and cook on the low setting (200°F — 100°C) for eight hours. Carve the chicken. Skim the fat from the sauce and pour over the chicken. Serve immediately.

Serves 4.

Chicken Casserole

1 chicken (3 lb - 1½ kg)	5½ tablespoons sherry
salt and pepper	¼ teaspoon tarragon
paprika	¼ teaspoon thyme
4 tablespoons (60 g) butter	½ lb (250 g) mushrooms,
⅔ cup (165 ml) chicken stock	sliced
2½ tablespoons chopped	4 teaspoons cornstarch
parsley	1 tablespoon water
1 clove garlic, minced	1 can (1 lb) artichoke hearts

1. Rub the outside of the chicken with salt, pepper and paprika. Brown on all sides in a frypan in one tablespoon butter. Put into the crockery pot.
2. Pour the chicken stock, parsley, garlic, sherry, tarragon and thyme into the frypan, scrape the bottom and cook for two minutes. Pour over the chicken.
3. Cover and cook on the low setting (200°F — 100°C) for eight hours. Remove from pot and keep warm.
4. Saute the mushrooms in the remaining butter. Add to the sauce with the cornstarch mixed with the water and the drained artichoke hearts. Turn to the high setting (300°F — 150°C) and cook, stirring constantly, until thickened. Pour over carved chicken.

Serves 4.

Chicken with White Wine

1 medium carrot, chopped	1 cup (250 ml) white wine
1 onion, chopped	1 cup (250 ml) chicken stock
3 tablespoons (45 g) butter	1 teaspoon tarragon
1 chicken (3 lb - 1½ kg)	salt and pepper
1 bay leaf	2 egg yolks
1½ tablespoons chopped	½ cup (125 ml) cream
parsley	

CONTINUED ON OPPOSITE PAGE

1. Saute the carrot and onion in the butter until the onion is transparent.
2. Add the chicken and brown well on all sides. Put the chicken with the carrot and onion into the crockery pot.
3. Add the bay leaf, parsley, white wine, chicken stock, tarragon and salt and pepper to taste.
4. Cover and cook on the low setting (200°F — 100°C) for eight hours. Remove chicken and keep warm.
5. Turn the heat up to the high setting (300°F — 150°C) and boil rapidly until the liquid is reduced to one cup.
6. Beat together the egg yolks and the cream. Add a little of the liquid to this mixture.
7. Turn the heat off and pour the egg yolks mixture into the crockery pot, stirring constantly.
8. Carve the chicken and pour the sauce over it.

Cherry Chicken

1 chicken (3 lb - 1½ kg)
3 tablespoons (45 g) butter
salt and pepper
1 cup (250 ml) chicken stock
½ cup chilli sauce

⅓ cup (85 ml) sherry
2 tablespoons cornstarch
4 tablespoons water
½ lb (250 g) dark red cherries, pitted

1. In a large frypan, brown the chicken in the butter on all sides. Season to taste with salt and pepper and put into the crockery pot.
2. Pour half the chicken stock into the frypan with the chilli sauce and scrape the bottom of the pan. Cook for one minute and pour over the chicken.
3. Cover and cook on the low setting (200°F — 100°C) for eight hours. Remove the chicken and keep warm.
4. Skim the fat from the liquid and turn the heat to the high setting.
5. Add the sherry and the cornflour mixed with the water. Stir until thick and smooth.
6. Add the cherries and heat thoroughly.
7. Cut the chicken into serving pieces and pour the cherry sauce over it.

Greek Lemon Chicken

1 chicken (3 lb - 1½ kg)	3 tablespoons (45 g) butter
salt and pepper	⅓ cup (85 ml) water
1 teaspoon oregano	¼ cup (65 ml) lemon juice
2 cloves garlic, minced	1 teaspoon grated lemon rind

1. Season the chicken inside and outside with salt and pepper.
2. Mix together half the oregano and one clove minced garlic and rub on the inside of the chicken.
3. Brown the chicken on all sides in the butter in a large frypan. Put the chicken in the crockery pot.
4. Sprinkle the chicken with the remaining oregano and garlic.
5. Add the water to the frypan and scrape the bottom. Pour over the chicken.
6. Cover and cook on the low setting (200°F — 100°C) for eight hours.
7. Mix together the lemon juice and grated rind and add to the chicken for the last hour of cooking.
8. Carve the chicken. Skim the fat from the sauce and pour over the chicken. Serve immediately.

Serves 4.

Fish

Salmon Poached in Wine

1 lb (500 g) salmon
2/3 cup (165 ml) white wine
1/2 cup (125 ml) water
1 bay leaf
4 tablespoons chopped celery
  leaves
1 small onion, chopped
1 teaspoon salt

4 teaspoons lemon juice
4 slices lemon
1/4 cup (65 g) butter
1/4 cup (65 ml) lemon juice
1 scallion, chopped
4 tablespoons minced parsley
1/4 teaspoon salt
1/4 teaspoon black pepper

1. Lay the salmon in the crockery pot.
2. Pour over the wine and water.
3. Add the bay leaf, celery leaves, onion, salt and lemon juice. Place the lemon slices on top.
4. Cover and cook on the low setting (200°F — 100°C) for two hours.
5. Melt the butter with the lemon juice, scallion, parsley, salt and pepper.
6. When the fish is cooked, strain and place on a serving dish. Pour the hot parsley butter over the fish and serve immediately.

Serves 3-4.

Italian Fish Stew

2 medium onions, chopped	2 cups (500 ml) water
5 tablespoons oil	salt and pepper
3 cloves garlic, minced	½ cup (125 ml) sherry
4 tablespoons chopped parsley	1 lb (500 g) fish fillets
	18 fresh clams, unshelled
1 lb (500 g) very ripe tomatoes	18 large fresh shrimp, unshelled
4 tablespoons tomato paste	

1. Saute the onions in the oil in a frypan until transparent.
2. Add the garlic and parsley and saute for a further two minutes. Put into the crockery pot.
3. Chop the tomatoes and add to the crockery pot with the tomato paste, water, salt and pepper to taste and the sherry. Mix thoroughly.
4. Cover and cook on the low setting (200°F — 100°C) for about two hours.
5. Cut the fish into bite size pieces and add to the crockery pot with the unshelled clams and shrimp.
6. Cover and cook on the high setting (300°F — 150°C) for about ½ hour or until the clams open.

Serves 6.

Scallops with Mushrooms

5 tablespoons (75 g) butter	2½ tablespoons dry sherry
5½ tablespoons white wine	1 lb (500 g) scallops
2½ tablespoons chopped parsley	½ lb (250 g) mushrooms, sliced
2 scallions, chopped	cooked rice

1. Combine the butter, wine, parsley, scallions and sherry in the crockery pot. Bring to a boil on the high setting (300°F — 150°C), stirring constantly.
2. Add the scallops and mushrooms. Cover and cook on the high setting for 15 minutes or until the scallops are tender.
3. Serve over hot rice.

Serves 4.

Stuffed Fish

1½ lb (750 g) fish fillets
salt and pepper
butter
½ lb (250 g) peeled shrimp
1 can cream of mushroom
  soup, undiluted

½ cup (125 ml) sherry
4 tablespoons lemon juice
⅓ cup grated Parmesan
  cheese
paprika
chopped chives

1. Season the fish fillets with salt and pepper to taste.
2. Put a teaspoon of butter on each fillet.
3. Chop the shrimp and spoon onto each fillet. Roll up and secure with tooth-picks. Put the rolls in a buttered crockery pot.
4. Mix together the soup, sherry and lemon juice in a saucepan. Bring to a simmer, stirring constantly.
5. Pour the sauce over the fish, sprinkle with cheese and a little paprika.
6. Cover and cook on the low setting (200°F — 100°C) for 1½ hours.
7. Serve garnished with chopped chives.

Serves 4.

Citrus Fish

1½ lb (750 g) fish fillets
salt and pepper
1 medium onion, chopped
5 tablespoons chopped
  parsley
4 teaspoons oil

2 teaspoons grated lemon
  rind
2 teaspoons grated orange
  rind
orange and lemon slices

1. Butter the crockery pot and place the fish fillets in it. Season to taste with salt and pepper.
2. Saute the onion and the chopped parsley in the oil until the onion is transparent. Sprinkle over the fish with the grated rinds.
3. Cover and cook on the low setting (200°F — 100°C) for 1½ hours.
4. Serve garnished with orange and lemon slices.

Serves 4.

Hungarian Fish

1½ lb (750 g) fish fillets
salt and pepper
1 cup (250 g) sour cream
3 teaspoons plain flour
1 medium onion, chopped

¼ cup (65 ml) white wine
1 teaspoon paprika
chopped parsley
lemon wedges

1. Season the fish fillets to taste with salt and pepper. Place the fish in a buttered crockery pot.
2. Blend together the sour cream, flour, onion and wine. Pour over the fish and sprinkle with paprika.
3. Cover and cook on the low setting (200°F — 100°C) for 1½ hours.
4. Serve garnished with chopped parsley and lemon wedges.

Serves 4.

Athenian Fish

½ lb (250 g) onions, sliced
¼ cup (65 ml) oil
½ lb (250 g) tomatoes
5 tablespoons chopped
   parsley
2 cloves garlic, minced

1½ lb (750 g) fish fillets
4 tablespoons lemon juice
salt and pepper
1 lemon, sliced
chopped chives

1. Saute the onions in the oil until golden brown.
2. Add half the tomatoes, the parsley and garlic. Cook for another five minutes.
3. Butter the crockery pot and place the fish on the bottom.
4. Sprinkle the lemon juice on the fish and season to taste with salt and pepper.
5. Pour the vegetables over the fish.
6. Slice the remaining tomatoes and place on top.
7. Put the lemon slices on top of the tomatoes.
8. Cover and cook on the low setting (200°F — 100°C) for 1½ hours. Garnish with chopped chives.

Serves 4.

Vegetables

Stuffed Cabbage

1 medium cabbage
1½ lb (750 g) ground veal or
  beef
1 cup cooked rice
1 egg, slightly beaten
1 medium onion, minced

1 medium carrot, grated
1½ teaspoons salt
¼ cup (65 ml) malt vinegar
½ cup brown sugar
1 can (400 g) tomatoes
4 teaspoons chopped chives

1. Put the whole cabbage in a large saucepan of boiling water for eight minutes.
   Drain and cool.
2. Remove eight to ten of the outer leaves. Remove the core and chop the rest of
   the cabbage.
3. Put the chopped cabbage on the bottom of the crockery pot.
4. Mix together the veal or beef, rice, egg, onion, carrot and salt.
5. Put a generous spoonful of this mixture on each cabbage leaf and roll towards
   the stem end, tucking in the sides as you roll.
6. Place the rolls on top of the chopped cabbage in the crockery pot.
7. Mix together the malt vinegar, sugar, chopped tomatoes and chives. Pour over
   the cabbage rolls.
8. Cover and cook on the low setting (200°F — 100°C) for eight to ten hours.

Serves 4-5.

Tomato Casserole

3 tablespoons (45 g) butter	4 teaspoons soy sauce
2 medium onions, chopped	¼ cup minced parsley
2 cloves garlic, minced	¼ cup (65 g) butter
½ lb (250 g) sausage meat	6 large tomatoes, thickly
1½ teaspoons salt	sliced
2 teaspoons brown sugar	¾ cup dried bread crumbs
½ cup dried bread crumbs	3 tablespoons (45 g) butter
¼ cup (65 ml) water	

1. Saute the onions and the garlic in the three tablespoons of butter until golden brown.
2. Add the sausage meat, salt and brown sugar and cook over a medium heat for four minutes, stirring constantly.
3. Combine the half cup of bread crumbs with the water mixed with the soy sauce. Add to the onion mixture. Mix well and remove from the heat.
4. Sprinkle on the parsley.
5. Spread the ¼ cup butter on the bottom and sides of the crockery pot.
6. Put a layer of tomato slices on the bottom and cover with a layer of the onion mixture. Repeat until all the ingredients are used up, ending with a layer of tomatoes.
7. Cover and cook on the low setting (200°F — 100°C) for six to eight hours.
8. Turn the tomato mixture into a baking dish and sprinkle with the ¾ cup of bread crumbs. Dot with the three tablespoons butter.
9. Place under a hot broiler and cook until the crumbs are golden brown.

Serves 6.

Zucchini Louisiana

2 lb (1 kg) zucchini
1 green pepper, chopped
1 medium onion, chopped
1 clove garlic, minced
1½ teaspoons salt

½ teaspoon black pepper
4 medium tomatoes, chopped
3 tablespoons (45 g) butter
2½ tablespoons chopped parsley

1. Slice the zucchini and combine with the green pepper, onion, garlic, salt and pepper in the crockery pot.
2. Top with the chopped tomatoes and dot with the butter.
3. Cover and cook on the high setting (300°F — 150°C) for two hours.
4. Serve sprinkled with chopped parsley.

Serves 6.

Ratatouille

⅓ cup (85 ml) oil
3 cloves garlic, minced
1 lb (500 g) tomatoes, quartered
1 eggplant, peeled and cubed
1 red pepper, sliced
1 green pepper, sliced
½ lb (250 g) zucchini, sliced

3 medium onions, quartered
½ lb (250 g) mushrooms, sliced
2 teaspoons salt
½ teaspoon pepper
½ teaspoon oregano
½ teaspoon basil

1. Saute the garlic in the oil for about two minutes. Put into the crockery pot.
2. Put the remaining ingredients into the crockery pot and mix thoroughly.
3. Cover and cook on the low setting (200°F — 100°C) for six to eight hours.
4. Before serving, remove the lid and turn the heat to the high setting (300°F — 150°C). Cook until all the liquid has gone.

Serves 8.

Potato-Onion Casserole

½ cup (125 ml) bacon fat
8 medium potatoes, sliced
4 medium onions, sliced
1 teaspoon salt
½ teaspoon pepper
chopped parsley

1. Saute the potatoes and onions in the bacon fat with the salt and pepper, stirring to coat the vegetables.
2. Put them into the crockery pot and cook on the low setting (200°F — 100°C) for four to six hours.
3. Serve sprinkled with chopped parsley.

Serves 8.

Vegetable Casserole with Chicken

2 cups chopped cooked chicken
3 medium carrots, sliced
2 stalks celery, sliced
1 turnip, sliced
1 sweet potato, diced
2 medium onions, chopped
4 medium potatoes, quartered
1 cup (250 ml) chicken stock

½ cup (125 ml) white wine
2 teaspoons salt
¼ teaspoon pepper
2½ tablespoons cold water
4 teaspoons cornstarch
2½ tablespoons lemon juice
2½ tablespoons chopped parsley
¼ teaspoon grated nutmeg
4 tablespoons cream

1. Put the chicken, carrots, celery, turnip, sweet potato, onions, potatoes, chicken stock, wine, salt and pepper into the crockery pot.
2. Cover and cook on the low setting (200°F — 100°C) for six to eight hours.
3. Pour the liquid from the crockery pot into a saucepan and place over a medium heat.
4. Mix together the water and cornstarch and slowly pour into the vegetable liquid, stirring constantly until the mixture thickens.
5. Add the lemon juice, parsley and nutmeg and cook for one minute, stirring constantly.
6. Stir in the cream and pour over the vegetables. Mix thoroughly and serve immediately.

Serves 6-8.

Braised Celery

12 large stalks celery
1 cup (250 ml) beef stock
½ teaspoon pepper
¼ cup (65 g) butter

1. Wash the celery well and cut into 3-inch (8-cm) lengths.
2. Put into the crockery pot with the beef stock and the pepper.
3. Cover and cook on the low setting (200°F — 100°C) for six to eight hours.
4. Remove celery from the crockery and keep warm.
5. Pour the stock into a small saucepan and boil rapidly until it is reduced to about ½ cup. Stir in the butter and cook until the butter is melted.
6. Pour the butter sauce over the celery and serve immediately.

Serves 4-6.

Braised Parsnips

8-10 medium parsnips,
  quartered
¼ cup (65 ml) chicken stock
1½ teaspoons salt
¼ cup (65 g) butter
1 teaspoon lemon juice

1. Put the parsnips in the crockery pot with the chicken stock and salt.
2. Cover and cook on the low setting (200°F — 100°C) for six to eight hours.
3. Uncover the crockery and turn the heat to the high setting (300°F — 150°C).
4. Add the butter and the lemon juice and cook until the butter is melted. Stir to ensure that the parsnips are well coated.

Serves 4-6.

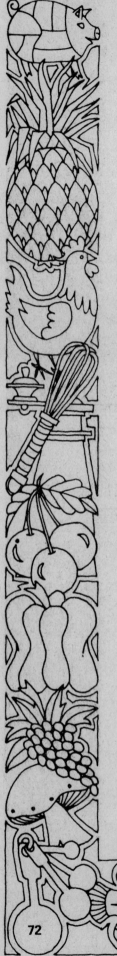

Tomato and Rice Casserole

4 teaspoons (20 g) butter
½ cup uncooked rice
1 cup (250 ml) liquid from canned tomatoes
1¾ cups canned tomatoes, drained

2 teaspoons chopped parsley
1½ teaspoons salt
½ teaspoon pepper
4 tablespoons grated Parmesan cheese
chopped chives

1. Saute the rice in the butter in a frypan until the rice is golden brown. Put into the crockery pot.
2. Pour the tomato liquid, tomatoes, parsley, salt and pepper into the crockery pot and mix well.
3. Cover and cook on the low setting (200°F — 100°C) for six to eight hours.
4. Sprinkle with Parmesan cheese and chopped chives before serving.

Serves 4.

Lima Beans with Sour Cream

1 lb (500 g) dried lima beans
6 cups (1½ liters) water
¼ cup (65 g) butter, melted
½ cup brown sugar
¼ cup (65 g) molasses

2½ tablespoons prepared mustard
1½ teaspoons salt
1 cup (250 g) sour cream

1. Soak the beans in the water overnight.
2. Cook in the same water in the crockery pot on the low setting (200°F — 100°C) for two to three hours. Drain.
3. Put the beans into a large bowl and add the butter, brown sugar, molasses, mustard and salt. Mix thoroughly.
4. Stir in the sour cream.
5. Put into a baking dish and bake in a 350°F (180°C) oven for about 40 minutes.

Serves 6-8.

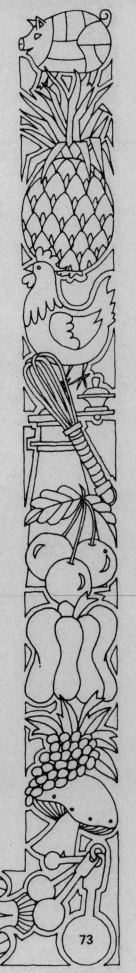

Bean Casserole

¾ lb (375 g) lean bacon,
  chopped
2 cloves garlic, minced
2 mediun onions, chopped
6 cups (1½ liters) water
1⅓ cups dried kidney beans
4 tablespoons brown sugar

2½ tablespoons prepared
  mustard
½ cup (125 ml) tomato sauce
½ cup (125 ml) red wine
1½ teaspoons salt
½ teaspoon pepper

1. Saute the bacon until crisp. Remove the bacon from the frypan.
2. Saute the garlic and onions in the bacon fat until transparent.
3. Add ½ cup of the water to the onions and cook over a low heat for one minute, scraping the bottom of the pan. Put into the crockery pot.
4. Add the remaining ingredients to the crockery pot with the cooked bacon. Mix well.
5. Cover and cook on the low setting (200°F — 100°C) for ten to twelve hours.

Serves 6-8.

Scalloped Potatoes

⅓ cup (85 g) butter
4 large potatoes, sliced
2½ teaspoons salt
½ teaspoon pepper
⅔ cup (165 ml) cream

1. Butter the bottom of the crockery pot.
2. Arrange the potatoes in layers, dotting each layer with butter and sprinkling with salt and pepper.
3. Pour the cream over the top.
4. Cover and cook on the high setting (300°F — 150°C) for three to four hours.

Serves 4.

Desserts and Cakes

Fresh Fruit Compote

10 plums
3 peaches
6 apricots
½ lb (250 g) seedless grapes
½ cup (125 ml) water
½ teaspoon cinnamon

½ cup sugar
4 teaspoons lemon juice
2½ tablespoons honey
1 lemon, sliced
sour cream

1. Peel and halve the plums, peaches and apricots. Remove the stems from the grapes.
2. In a small saucepan mix together the water, cinnamon and sugar. Heat until sugar is dissolved.
3. Add the honey and the lemon juice.
4. Put the fruit in the crockery pot and pour the syrup over it.
5. Put the lemon slices on top of the fruit.
6. Cover and cook on the low setting (200°F — 100°C) for about six hours.
7. Serve warm or chilled topped with a spoonful of sour cream.

Serves 6.

Poached Cherries

⅔ cup sugar
¾ cup (185 ml) water
1½ lb (750 g) cherries, pitted
4 tablespoons currant jam
ice cream or cream

1. Mix together the sugar and water in the crockery pot.
2. Cook the mixture on the high setting (300°F — 150°C) until the sugar is dissolved.
3. Add the cherries and the jam. Stir well.
4. Cover and cook for about ½ hour or until the cherries are tender.
5. Serve with cream or ice cream.

Serves 6.

Compote of Dried Fruit

½ lb (250 g) dried apricots
½ lb (250 g) dried apples
½ cup raisins
¼ cup currants
2½ cups (625 ml) water

¼ cup brown sugar
½ cup (125 ml) sherry
4 tablespoons lemon juice
vanilla ice cream
chopped walnuts

1. Mix together the apricots, apples, raisins, currants, water, brown sugar, sherry and lemon juice in the crockery pot.
2. Cover and cook on the low setting (200°F — 100°C) for about 3½ hours. Cool.
3. Place a scoop of ice cream in each dessert dish and spoon over the fruit. Top with chopped walnuts.

Serves 6.

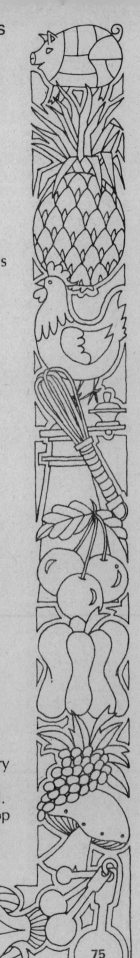

Port Plums

2 orange slices, quartered
8 whole cloves
1½ lb (750 g) plums, pitted
1 cup (250 ml) port
½ cup sugar
1 teaspoon cinnamon

1. Stick the cloves in the orange slices and put into the crockery pot with the plums, port, sugar and cinnamon.
2. Turn the crockery pot to the high setting (300°F — 150°C) and cook, uncovered, until the sugar dissolves.
3. Turn to the low setting (200°F — 100°C), cover and cook for about 1½ hours or until fruit is just tender.
4. Serve chilled.

Serves 6-8.

Orange Prunes

1 lb (500 g) pitted prunes
1 cup (250 ml) orange juice
2½ tablespoons lemon juice
1 teaspoon cinnamon
1 lemon, sliced

1. Place the prunes on the bottom of the crockery pot.
2. Pour on the orange juice and lemon juice.
3. Sprinkle on the cinnamon.
4. Place the lemon slices on top. (If the prunes are not completely covered with liquid, add a little more juice.)
5. Cover and cook on the low setting (200°F — 100°C) for about eight hours.

Serves 6.

Papaya with Ginger

1 large or 2 small papaya
¼ cup (65 g) butter
2 tablespoons lemon juice
2 teaspoons grated fresh
  ginger

1. Cut the papaya in quarters if it is large, in halves if they are small. Scoop out the seeds.
2. Mix together the butter, lemon juice and ginger in a small saucepan. Heat, stirring constantly, until the butter is melted.
3. Spoon the ginger mixture in the cavities of the papayas.
4. Cover and cook on the high setting (300°F — 150°C) for about 1½ hours or until they are tender. Baste occasionally during the cooking time. Serve warm.

Serves 4.

Pears with Wine

1 cup (250 ml) red wine
½ cup sugar
6 pears
12 cloves

1. Mix together the wine and sugar in the crockery pot.
2. Heat on the high setting (300°F — 150°C) until the sugar dissolves.
3. Core the pears but leave whole and do not peel.
4. Stick two cloves in each pear and place in the crockery pot.
5. Cover and cook on the low setting (200°F — 100°C) for about 3½ hours. Baste occasionally. Serve warm or cold.

Serves 6.

Beer Cake

⅔ cup (165 g) butter	½ teaspoon salt
1½ cups brown sugar	1 teaspoon cinnamon
3 eggs	¼ teaspoon nutmeg
2½ cups plain flour	1½ cups (375 ml) beer
1½ teaspoons baking powder	1 cup chopped walnuts
½ teaspoon baking soda	1 cup raisins

1. Cream together the butter and sugar until light and fluffy.
2. Add the eggs and beat well.
3. Sift together the flour, baking powder, baking soda, salt, cinnamon and nutmeg and add to the creamed mixture alternately with the beer.
4. Stir in the walnuts and raisins.
5. Pour the mixture into a well-buttered and floured cake tin that will fit into the crockery pot. Cover the tin with four to five layers of paper towels. Put into the crockery pot.
6. Put the lid of the crockery pot on loosely to allow the steam to escape and cook on the high setting (300°F — 150°C) for about 3½ hours or until the cake is cooked.
7. Remove from the crockery pot and allow to cool on a wire rack for 15 minutes before removing from the tin.

Apricot-Almond Dessert

1 lb (500 g) fresh apricots
½ cup brown sugar
½ cup (125 ml) water
3 teaspoons butter

2½ tablespoons sugar
½ cup slivered almonds
vanilla ice cream

1. Plunge the apricots into boiling water for 30 seconds. Remove, cool slightly and peel. Cut the apricots in half and remove the stone. Place in the crockery pot.
2. Sprinkle the brown sugar over the apricots.
3. Pour on the water.
4. Cover and cook on the low setting (200°F — 100°C) for about 1½ hours or until the apricots are tender. Keep warm.
5. In a saucepan, mix together the butter and sugar. Heat until both are melted.
6. Add the almonds and stir until they are completely coated with the caramelized sugar.
7. Put a scoop of vanilla ice cream in individual dessert dishes. Spoon on the apricots and top with the nuts. Serve immediately.

Serves 6.

Baked Apples

6 large cooking apples
¾ cup (185 ml) orange juice
2 teaspoons grated orange
   rind
1 teaspoon grated lemon rind

¾ cup (185 ml) rose wine
¼ teaspoon cinnamon
½ cup brown sugar
whipped cream

1. Remove the core from the apples and place them in the crockery pot.
2. Mix together the orange juice, orange rind, lemon rind, rose wine, cinnamon and sugar. Pour over the apples.
3. Cover the crockery pot and cook on the low setting (200°F — 100°C) for about 3½ hours or until the apples are tender.
4. Serve smothered with whipped cream.

Serves 6.

Applesauce Cake

½ cup (125 g) butter
1 cup sugar
2 eggs
1 teaspoon vanilla essence
1 cup applesauce
1½ teaspoons baking soda

1½ cups plain flour
1 teaspoon cinnamon
½ teaspoon salt
¼ teaspoon nutmeg
¾ cup chopped dates
¾ cup chopped walnuts

1. Cream together the butter and sugar until light and fluffy.
2. Add the eggs and beat well.
3. Add the vanilla essence, and applesauce.
4. Sift together the baking soda, flour, cinnamon, salt and nutmeg. Add to the mixture and beat until smooth.
5. Fold in the dates and walnuts.
6. Pour the mixture into a well-buttered and floured cake tin that will fit into the crockery pot. Put into the crockery pot and cover with four to five layers of paper towels.
7. Cover the crockery pot loosely to allow steam to escape and cook on the high setting (300°F — 150°C) for about 3½ hours or until the cake is cooked.
8. Remove from the crockery pot and allow the cake to cool on a wire rack for 15 minutes before removing from the tin.

Carrot Pudding

1 cup plain flour	⅓ cup (85 g) butter
1 cup brown sugar	1 egg
1 teaspoon baking soda	1 cup grated carrots
1½ teaspoons cinnamon	1 cup grated apples
½ teaspoon nutmeg	½ cup raisins
½ teaspoon ground cloves	¼ cup currants

1. Sift together flour, sugar, baking soda, cinnamon, nutmeg and cloves.
2. Add the butter and egg and mix until smooth.
3. Blend in the carrots, apples, raisins and currants.
4. Pour into a well-buttered and floured basin that will fit into the crockery pot.
5. Pour two cups of water into the crockery pot.
6. Cover the basin with aluminum foil and place into the crockery pot.
7. Cover the crockery pot with aluminum foil, then put on the lid.
8. Cook on the high setting (300°F — 150°C) for about four or five hours. Serve warm.

Serves 6-8.

Sliced Apples

8 large cooking apples
½ cup (125 ml) water
¾ cup sugar
1 teaspoon cinnamon
½ teaspoon nutmeg
ice cream

1. Peel, slice and core the apples.
2. Lightly butter the bottom of the crockery pot and put in the apples slices.
3. Pour on the water and sprinkle the sugar mixed with the cinnamon and nutmeg on top.
4. Cover and cook on the low setting (200°F — 100°C) for about 3½ hours.
5. Serve warm or cold with vanilla ice cream.

Serves 6-8.

Date Bread

1 cup (250 ml) boiling water
1 cup chopped dates
3 eggs, lightly beaten
1 cup brown sugar
1 cup plain flour
¼ cup wheat germ

1 teaspoon baking powder
½ teaspoon baking soda
¼ teaspoon salt
2 cups all-bran cereal
1 cup chopped walnuts

1. Pour the boiling water over the dates and leave until cool.
2. Beat together the eggs and sugar until thick.
3. Add the dates and mix well.
4. Mix together the flour, wheat germ, baking powder, baking soda and salt.
5. Add to the egg and sugar mixture and blend thoroughly.
6. Stir in the cereal and walnuts.
7. Pour the mixture into a well-buttered and floured tube tin that fits into the crockery pot.* Put into crockery pot.
8. Put the lid of the crockery pot on loosely to allow steam to escape. Cook on the high setting (300°F — 150°C) for about three hours or until cooked.

*A large soup tin or a coffee tin are suitable. In this case cover the top of the tin with several layers of paper towels.

Health Bread

1 cup whole wheat flour	½ cup brown sugar
1 cup plain flour	4 tablespoons molasses
1 cup corn meal	¼ cup (65 g) butter
½ cup wheat germ	2 cups (500 ml) buttermilk
1 teaspoon baking powder	1 cup raisins
1 teaspoon baking soda	
1 teaspoon salt	

1. Mix together the wheat flour, plain flour, corn meal, wheat germ, baking powder, baking soda, salt and brown sugar in a mixing bowl.
2. Add the molasses, butter and buttermilk and mix well.
3. Stir in the raisins.
4. Pour the mixture into a well-buttered and floured tin that will fit into the crockery pot. Cover with aluminum foil.
5. Pour two cups of water into the crockery, then put in the filled tin.
6. Cover the crockery pot and cook on the high setting (300°F — 150°C) for about four hours or until the bread is cooked.

Banana Bread

⅔ cup (165 g) butter	¼ cup wheat germ
1 cup sugar	½ teaspoon cinnamon
2 eggs	½ teaspoon salt
1 cup mashed bananas	1 teaspoon baking soda
1 cup whole wheat flour	½ cup chopped walnuts
1 cup plain flour	

1. Cream together the butter and sugar until light and fluffy.
2. Add the eggs and bananas and mix thoroughly.
3. Mix together the whole wheat flour, plain flour, wheat germ, cinnamon, salt and baking soda. Add to the banana mixture. Fold in walnuts.
4. Pour into a well-buttered and floured tin that will fit into the crockery pot. Cover with several layers of paper towels. Put into the crockery pot.
5. Cover the crockery pot loosely to allow the steam to escape and cook on the high setting (300°F — 150°C) for three to four hours or until cooked.

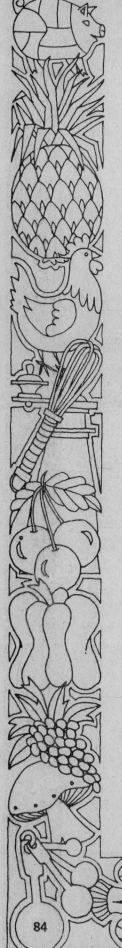

Orange-Date Cake

¼ cup (65 g) butter
1 cup sugar
1 egg
2 cups plain flour
1 teaspoon baking powder

1 teaspoon baking soda
½ teaspoon salt
1 cup (250 ml) orange juice
1 cup chopped dates

1. Cream together the butter and sugar until light and fluffy.
2. Add the egg and beat well.
3. Sift together the flour, baking powder, baking soda and salt.
4. Add the sifted dry ingredients alternately with the orange juice to the butter-sugar-egg mixture.
5. Gently stir in the dates.
6. Pour the mixture into a well-buttered and floured tin that fits into the crockery pot. Put into the crockery pot. Cover with four to five layers of paper towels.
7. Cover the crockery pot loosely to allow steam to escape.
8. Cook on the high setting (300°F — 150°C) for about 3½ hours or until the cake is cooked.
9. Cool for 15 minutes before removing from tin.

Chocolate Chip Cake

½ cup (125 g) butter
1 cup sugar
2 eggs
1 cup (250 ml) cream
1½ teaspoons vanilla essence

2½ cups plain flour
1 teaspoon baking powder
1 teaspoon baking soda
½ teaspoon salt
6 oz (185 g) chocolate bits

1. Cream together the butter and sugar until light and fluffy.
2. Add the eggs and beat well.
3. Mix in the cream and vanilla essence.
4. Sift together the flour, baking powder, baking soda and salt and add to the creamed mixture.
5. Fold in the chocolate bits.
6. Pour into a well-buttered and floured cake tin that will fit into the crockery pot. Cover the top of the tin with four to five layers of paper towels.
7. Cover the crockery pot loosely to allow the steam to escape and cook on the high setting (300°F — 150°C) for four to five hours or until the cake is cooked.
8. Allow to cook for 15 minutes on a wire rack before removing from the tin.

Chocolate Mashed Potato Cake

⅔ cup (165 g) butter
1½ cups sugar
4 eggs, slightly beaten
1 cup mashed potatoes
2 cups plain flour
1 teaspoon salt

⅔ cup cocoa
2 teaspoons baking powder
1 teaspoon cinnamon
¼ teaspoon nutmeg
½ cup (125 ml) milk
½ cup chopped walnuts

1. Cream together the butter and sugar until light and fluffy.
2. Add the eggs and beat well.
3. Stir in the mashed potatoes.
4. Add the sifted dry ingredients alternately with the milk.
5. Fold in the nuts.
6. Pour the mixture into a well-buttered and flour tin that will fit into the crockery pot. Cover the tin with four to five layers of paper towels.
7. Cover the crockery pot loosely so that the steam can escape.
8. Cook on the high setting (300°F — 150°C) for about 3½ hours or until the cake is cooked.
9. Cool for 15 minutes before removing from the tin.

Fig Pudding

1 lb (500 g) dried figs	½ cup sugar
2½ tablespoons plain flour	2 eggs
1 cup (250 g) butter	1 teaspoon baking soda
1 cup light molasses	3 cups cake flour
¾ cup (185 ml) cold milk	½ teaspoon salt
1 teaspoon grated lemon rind	
1 teaspoon grated orange rind	

1. Chop the figs finely with two tablespoons of the flour. Keep dipping the knife into the flour to prevent the figs from sticking together.
2. Mix in the butter and the remaining ingredients.
3. Pour into a well-buttered and floured dish that will fit into the crockery pot. Cover loosely with aluminum foil.
4. Put into the crockery pot, cover and cook on the low setting (200°F — 100°C) for six to eight hours.

Serves 6-8.

Cornbread

1¼ cups plain flour	1 teaspoon salt
¾ cup cornmeal	1 egg, lightly beaten
¼ cup sugar	1 cup (250 ml) milk
4 teaspoons baking powder	⅓ cup (85 ml) melted butter

1. Mix together the flour, cornmeal, sugar, baking powder and salt.
2. Beat together the egg, milk and melted butter. Stir into the flour mixture until just moistened.
3. Pour into a well-buttered and floured tin that will fit into the crockery pot. Cover with a plate and put into the crockery pot.
4. Cover and cook on the high setting (300°F — 150°C) for two to three hours.

Serves 6.

Rhubarb Delight

4 cups 2-inch (5-cm) pieces
rhubarb
¾ cup sugar
½ cup (125 ml) water

3 tablespoons (45 g) butter
½ teaspoon vanilla essence
2 cups (500 ml) cream,
whipped

1. Put the rhubarb into the crockery pot with the sugar and water.
2. Cover and cook on the low setting (200°F — 100°C) for six to eight hours.
3. Turn off the heat and drain off most of the liquid.
4. Stir in the butter and vanilla essence. Cool.
5. Fold in the whipped cream and chill well in the refrigerator before serving.

Serves 8.

Stewed Apricots

1 lb (500 g) dried apricots
3 cups (750 ml) water
1½ tablespoons grated orange
rind
2 teaspoons grated lemon
rind

2½ tablespoons orange
marmalade
4 teaspoons Cointreau

1. Put the apricots, water, orange rind, lemon rind and marmalade into the crockery pot.
2. Cover and cook on the low setting (200°F — 100°C) for ten to twelve hours.
3. Cool the apricots, then chill in the refrigerator.
4. Stir in the Cointreau just before serving.

Serves 6.

Walnut-Raisin Cake

1 cup raisins	1½ cups plain flour
¾ cup (185 ml) boiling water	1½ teaspoons baking soda
¼ cup (65 g) butter	½ teaspoon salt
2 eggs, beaten	¾ cup chopped walnuts
1 teaspoon vanilla essence	
1 cup sugar	

1. Pour the boiling water over the raisins, add the butter and mix well. Set aside.
2. Mix together the eggs, vanilla essence and sugar in a large mixing bowl.
3. Combine the flour, baking soda and salt and stir into the egg mixture.
4. Add the raisin mixture and mix until just blended.
5. Fold in the walnuts.
6. Pour the mixture into a well-buttered and floured cake tin that will fit into the crockery pot. Cover the tin with four to five layers of paper towels and put into the crockery pot.
7. Put the lid on the crockery pot loosely to allow the steam to escape. Cook on the high setting (300°F — 150°C) for four to six hours.
8. Cool on a rack for 15 minutes before removing from the tin.

Rice Pudding

4 cups (1 liter) milk
1 cup cooked rice
3 eggs, lightly beaten
½ cup sugar
2 teaspoons vanilla essence
½ cup raisins
1½ teaspoons grated lemon
    rind

½ teaspoon nutmeg
½ teaspoon cinnamon
3 tablespoons (45 g) butter
4 tablespoons dark rum
whipped cream

1. Warm the milk slightly and pour over the rice. Set aside.
2. Beat the eggs with the sugar, vanilla essence, raisins and lemon rind.
3. Stir in the milk and rice mixture.
4. Put into a well-buttered souffle dish that will fit into the crockery pot.
5. Sprinkle with nutmeg and cinnamon and dot with the butter.
6. Cover with aluminum foil and put into the crockery pot.
7. Cover the crockery pot and cook on the low setting (200°F — 100°C) for four to six hours.
8. Put the rice pudding into a serving dish and stir in the rum.
9. Serve warm topped with whipped cream.

Serves 6.

Bread Pudding

4 eggs, beaten
1 cup (250 ml) milk
1 cup (250 ml) cream
½ cup sugar
1 teaspoon vanilla essence

¼ teaspoon salt
5 cups cubed, buttered stale
    white bread
¼ cup (65 ml) dry sherry
1 cup sultanas

1. Beat together the egg, milk, cream, sugar, vanilla essence and salt.
2. Mix with the bread cubes and allow to stand for 15-20 minutes.
3. Put a layer of the bread cube mixture on the bottom of a well-buttered baking dish that will fit into the crockery pot.
4. Sprinkle a little of the sherry and a layer of the sultanas over the bread cubes. Continue until all ingredients are used ending with a layer of bread cubes.
5. Cover the tin with aluminum foil and put into the crockery pot.
6. Pour ½ cup (125 ml) water into the crockery pot, put on the lid and cook on the high setting (300°F — 150°C) for two to three hours.

Serves 6.

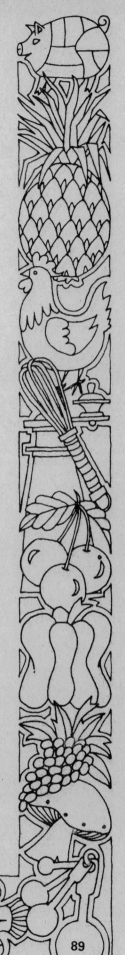

Apple Cake

1 cup plain flour	4 cups sliced cooking apples
1½ teaspoons baking powder	1 teaspoon cinnamon
½ teaspoon salt	½ teaspoon nutmeg
4 teaspoons sugar	2½ tablespoons brown sugar
¼ cup (65 g) butter	½ cup orange marmalade
1 egg, lightly beaten	2½ tablespoons melted butter
¼ cup (65 ml) milk	

1. Sift together the flour, baking powder, salt and sugar into a mixing bowl.
2. Rub in the butter until the mixture resembles bread crumbs.
3. Add the egg and milk and mix until smooth.
4. Pour the mixture into a well-buttered and floured cake tin that will fit into the crockery pot.
5. Arrange the apple slices on top and press them into the batter.
6. Mix together the cinnamon, nutmeg and brown sugar. Sprinkle over the cake.
7. Dot with marmalade and drip the butter over all.
8. Put the lid loosely on the crockery pot to allow the steam to escape. Cook on the high setting (300°F — 150°C) for six to eight hours. Serve warm with whipped cream.

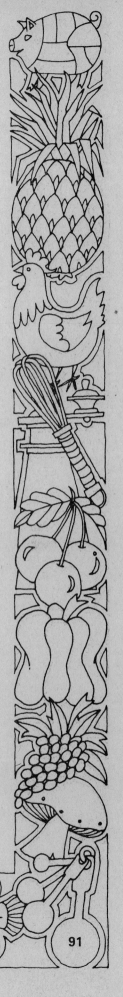

Apricot-Nut Cake

¾ cup dried apricots
1 cup plain flour
2 teaspoons baking powder
¼ teaspoon baking soda
½ teaspoon salt
½ cup sugar
¾ cup (185 ml) milk

1 egg, lightly beaten
4 teaspoons grated orange rind
4 teaspoons oil
½ cup whole wheat flour
1 cup chopped walnuts

1. Sprinkle the apricots with one tablespoon of the flour and chop them finely with a floured knife. Keep dipping the knife in the flour to prevent the apricots from sticking together.
2. Sift together the remaining flour, the baking powder, baking soda, salt and sugar into a large bowl.
3. Mix together the milk, egg, orange rind and oil. Pour into the flour mixture with the whole wheat flour and mix well.
4. Fold in the apricots with the flour from the chopping board and the walnuts.
5. Pour into a well-buttered and floured cake tin that will fit into the crockery pot. Cover with four layers of paper towels.
6. Place the cake tin in the crockery pot and cover loosely with the lid to allow the steam to escape.
7. Cook on the high setting (300°F — 150°C) for four to six hours.
8. Cool on a rack for 15 minutes before removing from the tin. Serve warm or cold.

Chocolate Pudding Cake

2 cups plain flour
2 teaspoons baking powder
¼ teaspoon salt
½ cup cocoa
½ cup (125 g) butter
½ cup sugar
4 eggs
1 cup (250 ml) milk
1½ cups fresh bread crumbs
1 teaspoon vanilla essence

1. Sift together the flour, baking powder, salt and cocoa.
2. Cream together the butter and sugar until light and fluffy.
3. Add the eggs one at a time alternating with the flour mixture. Beat well.
4. Beat in the milk, vanilla and the bread crumbs.
5. Pour into a well-buttered and floured baking dish that will fit into the crockery pot. Cover with aluminum foil and place on a rack in the crockery pot.
6. Pour in two cups (500 ml) hot water and cover the crockery pot. Cook on the high setting (300°F — 150°C) for three to four hours.

Serves 6.

Stewed Prunes

1 lb (500 g) dried prunes,
  unpitted
3 cups (750 ml) water
peel of ¼ lemon, cut in strips
1 teaspoon vanilla essence
whipped cream

1. Put the prunes, water and lemon rind into the crockery pot.
2. Cover and cook on the low setting (200°F — 100°C) for ten to twelve hours.
3. Stir in the vanilla and cool slightly before serving.
4. Serve with whipped cream.

Serves 6.

Plum Pudding

4 slices bread, cut up
1 cup (250 ml) milk
2 eggs, lightly beaten
1 cup brown sugar
¼ cup (65 ml) orange juice
6 oz (185 g) finely chopped
  suet
1 teaspoon vanilla essence
1 cup plain flour
1 teaspoon baking soda

½ teaspoon salt
2 teaspoons cinnamon
1 teaspoon ground cloves
1 teaspoon mace
1 cup currants
1 cup raisins
1 cup chopped dates
½ cup chopped mixed peel
½ cup walnuts

1. Soak the bread in the milk until the milk is completely absorbed.
2. Beat in the eggs, sugar, orange juice, suet and vanilla.
3. In a large bowl mix together the flour, baking soda, salt, cinnamon, cloves and mace.
4. Stir in the fruits and nuts.
5. Add the bread mixture and mix thoroughly.
6. Pour into a well-buttered and floured enamel mold that fits into the crockery pot. Cover with aluminum foil and secure with string.
7. Put into the crockery pot with one inch (2½ cm) of water.
8. Cover and cook on the high setting (300°F — 150°C) for six hours. Cool for 15 minutes before removing from the mold.

Serves 10.

Blueberry Cake

2 cups plain flour	1 cup (250 ml) milk
3 teaspoons baking powder	½ cup (125 g) butter, melted
1 teaspoon salt	1 cup blueberries
2½ tablespoons sugar	4 tablespoons sugar
1 egg, lightly beaten	

1. Sift together the flour, baking powder, salt and sugar into a mixing bowl.
2. Add the egg, milk and butter and stir until just blended.
3. Mix the blueberries with the sugar and fold into the cake mixture.
4. Pour the batter into a well-buttered and floured cake tin that will fit into the crockery pot. Cover the tin with four or five layers of paper towels and put into the crockery pot.
5. Put the lid on the crockery pot loosely to allow the steam to escape and cook on the low setting (200°F — 100°C) for four to six hours.

Index

Italian Beef Stew 40
Italian Fish Stew 64

Lamb Chops with Prunes 49
Lamb Curry 51
Lamb Meat Balls 49
Lamb Meat Loaf 46
Lamb Shank Stew 43
Lentil Soup 21
Lima Beans with Sour Cream 72

Meat and Bean Stew 50
Meat Loaf 39
Mexican Soup 13
Moroccan Veal Stew 31
Mulligatawny Soup 22

New England Corned Beef 51
Noodle Meat Casserole 30

Onion Soup 15
Orange Chicken 56
Orange-Date Cake 84
Orange Pork Chops 47
Orange Prunes 76

Papaya with Ginger 77
Paprika Beef 45
Pears with Wine 77
Plum Pudding 93
Poached Cherries 75
Poached Chicken 54
Pork and Beans 34
Pork with Pears 36
Port Plums 76
Potato-Onion Casserole 70

Quick and Easy Mixed Soup 11

Rabbit Chasseur 52
Ratatouille 69
Red Chicken 54
Rhubarb Delight 87
Rice Pudding 89

Salmon Poached in Wine 63
Scalloped Potatoes 73
Scallops with Mushrooms 64
Simple Veal Stew 31
Sliced Apples 81
Spicy Frankfurters 32
Spinach Meat Balls 24
Split Pea Soup 21
Stewed Apricots 87
Stewed Prunes 93
Stuffed Breast of Lamb 33
Stuffed Breast of Veal 34

Stuffed Cabbage 67
Stuffed Chicken 59
Stuffed Fish 65
Swedish Meat Balls 28
Swiss Steak 28

Three-Meat Stew 41
Tomato and Rice Casserole 72
Tomato Casserole 68
Tongue with Port Sauce 48
Topside Roast with Sour cream Sauce 47

Veal Paprika 32
Veal Pot Roast 35
Vegetable Casserole with Chicken 70
Vegetable Soup 16
Veal Stew with Wine 42
Vichyssoise 17

Walnut Beef 26
Walnut-Raisin Cake 88

Yellow Split Pea Soup 12

Zucchini Louisiana 69

FR-B8096-3/69